THE COMPLETE GUIDE TO
PET AND AVIARY
BIRD CARE

DAVID ALDERTON

ANIMAL CARE

THE COMPLETE GUIDE TO
PET AND AVIARY
BIRD CARE

MITCHELL BEAZLEY

Executive Art Editor: Emma Boys
Executive Editor: Samantha Ward-Dutton
Produced for Mitchell Beazley by **PAGE***One*
Cairn House, Elgiva Lane, Chesham, Buckinghamshire HP5 2JD
Production: Paul Hammond

First published in Great Britain in 1998 by Mitchell Beazley,
an imprint of Reed Consumer Books Limited
Michelin House, 81 Fulham Road, London SW3 6RB

ISBN 1-84000-038-4

A CIP catalogue of this book is available at the British Library.

Printed in Singapore

Contents

Introduction

Few hobbies are more relaxing or offer greater scope than bird-keeping, which is now a popular pastime worldwide. But bird-keeping is not a new hobby. More than 2000 years ago, the ancient Egyptians were already keeping birds, including parrots, in traditional rectangular cages; in India, the mynah was prized for its ability to talk; and the ancient Greeks were breeding and selling peacocks, which were highly valued for their iridescent plumage. As early civilizations explored new lands, new species were discovered, and some, such as the budgerigar, which comes originally from Australia, have become very popular as pets. These small parakeets are easy to tame and make ideal talking companions. Equally, they can be easily housed in a garden aviary, or even raised as exhibition birds. This versatility has led to the budgerigar replacing the canary as the most popular pet bird in the world.

Whether you are seeking a talking companion, a colourful songster or a large collection for a garden aviary there is a tremendous range of birds from which to choose, from tiny jewel-like finches and red and yellow canaries, to vivid macaws and chattering grey parrots. Whatever your circumstances, you are likely to find a bird that appeals to you in this book.

Parrots make popular, long-lived companions, and are noted for their loyalty, an ability to talk, and lively antics.

Choosing birds

This book profiles more than 50 of the most attractive, popular, and easy-to-keep birds and includes representatives of all the major groups, ranging from widely kept softbills, finches, and canaries to budgerigars, lovebirds, cockatiels, and large parrots. The text is accompanied by full-colour photographs, and special summaries and key symbols combine to show the conditions each species requires, enabling you to decide on the type of set-up that you will need for your birds. Guidance on compatibility and detailed breeding information are also provided. The symbols here will enable you to recognize whether a particular species will settle well as a pet, rather than simply as a breeding bird in aviary surroundings.

Preparing for a new bird

Before you acquire a new bird, it is important to have accommodation and equipment ready. Spend time studying the different designs of cages and aviaries that are currently available and establish your choice well in advance of bringing your bird home. You can then take time selecting your bird without feeling pressured.

It is vital to select as large a cage or aviary as possible, so as to give your birds plenty of space. This will be especially important if the birds will not be able to spend much time out of their quarters. With adequate space birds are likely to remain fitter and live longer.

Purchasing an aviary is an expensive undertaking, so it is important to choose a design that fits in with your plans at the outset. Any mistakes made at this early stage can prove to be very costly in the long term.

When it then comes to selecting the birds themselves, the advice given in the following pages should help to simplify the process, ensuring that you can recognize the key signs of health without difficulty.

Caring for birds

It is always advisable to buy new birds from reputable owners or breeders and to be aware of what to look for to ensure the birds you choose are healthy. You will also need to equip yourself with a suitable carrying box so you can transport your bird to its new home. Once you arrive, there are special techniques for safely catching and handling different types of bird. You also need to know what type of food to provide to keep your bird or birds in top condition.

Some birds thrive better in the openness of an outdoor aviary and prefer to live in flocks.

Breeding birds

All types of birds can now be bred in aviaries, and there have been significant advances in this field over recent years, many of which are discussed in depth in this book. As well as explaining the complexities of genetics and colour breeding, helpful advice is given on making preparations for the breeding season, nesting, and rearing and weaning chicks successfully by hand. Practical information on special diets, equipment, and the importance of keeping chicks warm and clean will enable you to hand-rear chicks with confidence, recognize problems, and deal with emergencies.

Healthy living

Detailed health care advice should help to ensure that your new pet thrives in its new home. Once they are established in their quarters, birds are generally very easy to look after, and rarely fall ill. However, the ability to recognize and act when you notice signs of sickness is vital, because, without proper attention, the condition of a sick bird can deteriorate rapidly to a point beyond hope of recovery. Information on when to seek help from a vet, to ensure that your pet has a long and healthy life, is therefore of the utmost importance.

Using this book

This book is intended as a sound guide for new bird-keepers, as well as a valuable handbook for more experienced owners. In writing it, I have placed great emphasis on the inclusion of details about the latest advances in bird care, covering topics such as diet, sexing, and hand-rearing, while not overlooking other relevant areas such as evolution and anatomy. The core guide to the breeds and species will serve as an ongoing reference point, providing an easily accessible source of information for all the key facts about a particular bird or group, should you wish to expand your interest.

The book follows a logical progression through the anatomy of birds and the history of bird-keeping, to practical considerations of what type of bird to choose, where to buy birds, suitable accommodation, and every aspect of bird care. By taking the time to read the book through, or simply dip into it for specific advice, you will learn to pre-empt problems and ensure that your bird or birds remain happy and healthy.

What is a bird?

For thousands of years, people have been fascinated by birds, which have changed little since their prehistoric ancestors took to the skies. Understanding how birds live and learning how to interpret their behaviour will greatly enhance your relationship with your pet and enable you to give it the very best care.

Development of birds

Until recently, the fossilized remains of a small bird-like reptile called *Archaeopteryx* were thought to represent the ancestral form of modern birds. This crow-sized creature, which lived during the Jurassic period 147 million years ago, had toothed jaws, clawed wings, and feathers. Although modern birds have no teeth, young hoatzins (*Opisthocomus hoatzin*), primitive birds found in the northern Amazon rain forests, have temporary wing claws, which they use to anchor themselves to branches until they can fly, after which the claws are shed. The clear evidence of feathers, which are a defining characteristic of birds, set *Archaeopteryx* apart from the dinosaurs, although its skeleton shows that it was not a good flier.

THE TRUE ANCESTORS OF BIRDS

Today, as a result of remarkable fossil finds in China in 1995, some scientists no longer believe *Archaeopteryx* to be the direct ancestor of birds, and claim it played no part in their evolution. These remains, which also date from the Jurassic, are clearly of a small bird, about the size of a warbler. The presence of a well-developed keel on the sternum or breastbone, to which the flight muscles attach, confirm that some birds were already actively flying at this time, rather than just gliding. Another Chinese fossil from the same period shows that the tail vertebrae (pygostyle) were already fused together to assist flight. All these features are present in modern birds, but absent in *Archaeopteryx*.

Their small size, frail skeletons and the fact that they were less likely to die in areas where fossilization might occur has limited our knowledge of the evolutionary history of birds, hence the continuing controversy over *Archaeopteryx*. We are not even sure how many separate lineages were involved in their early development.

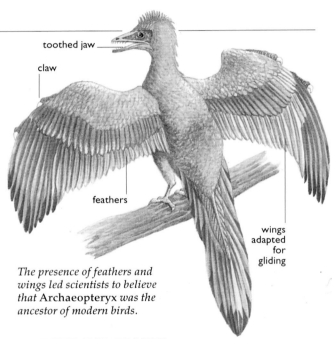

toothed jaw

claw

feathers

wings adapted for gliding

The presence of feathers and wings led scientists to believe that **Archaeopteryx** *was the ancestor of modern birds.*

ADAPTED FOR FLIGHT

The basic design of a bird's body has not changed dramatically since the first prehistoric birds that took to the air during the Jurassic. However, flight imposes very demanding criteria on the engineering of the body, which must be equipped with large wings, powerful muscles, a specially adapted skeleton, and weigh as little as possible.

The forearms of the bird have become modified into wings to provide the propulsive thrust that is needed for flight. This is achieved by having a relatively large surface area, which is increased by the presence of modified, elongated flight feathers that run down the rear edge of each wing.

The power that a bird needs in order to be able to fly is provided by the muscles that run from wing to wing on the underside of the body. The prominent breastbone or sternum serves as the main surface of attachment for these muscles. Secondary points of attachment are the collar bones, which have become fused in front of the sternum, providing additional support.

The flight muscles can account for up to one-third of the bird's total bodyweight. To provide the space necessary to accommodate them, the shoulder joints have moved vertically through evolution, and now lie alongside the vertebral column.

Low bodyweight helps to reduce the muscular effort necessary for flight and this is clearly evident in a bird's skeleton. The teeth and related muscles have disappeared from the jaws, and the long tail, now redundant since birds can use their wings to steer themselves in the air, has become shortened to form the pygostyle, to which the tail feathers are attached.

Birds are warm-blooded, like mammals, but have an even higher body temperature, which is typically more than 37.7°C (100°F). Their light plumage offers an effective way of retaining heat. It also avoids the need for an insulating layer of body fat beneath the skin, which would increase their bodyweight unnecessarily.

TYPES OF FEATHER

A bird's plumage includes three main types of feather. The main body is covered in contour feathers, beneath which is a soft layer of downy feathers to trap warm air and maintain body temperature. Long flight feathers on the wings are necessary for flying. The feathers are replaced regularly during the moulting period.

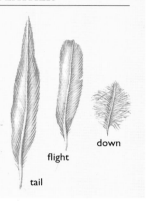

down

flight

tail

WALKING AND WADDLING

The length of the wings and the physical thrust that is required for a bird to take off in flight have affected the structure and positioning of the legs. To prevent a bird from falling over, the centre of gravity lies between the legs, at the point where the keel of the sternum extends. This is what gives birds their characteristic waddling gait.

The legs themselves are powerful, and are particularly useful in helping a bird spring into the air. Above the legs, the hip joint has become significantly enlarged so that it can provide for the muscles attached to the limb bones. While the hips have become tightly bound against the vertebral column, in the front part of the body the keel is held away from the shoulders by large coracoid bones, to allow for the contraction of the flight muscles. Similarly, the keel is supported by ribs, which encase the body cavity and body organs.

Unlike mammals, birds lack a diaphragm which acts as a partition between the chest and the abdomen.

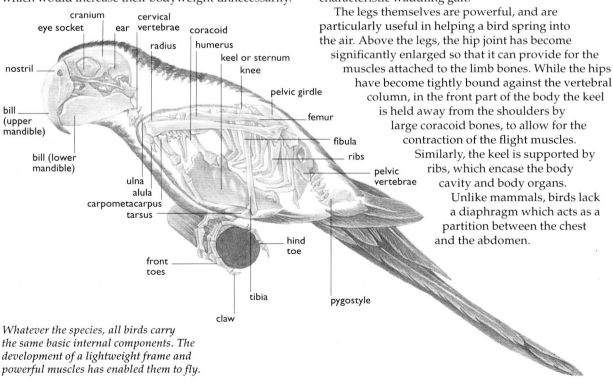

Whatever the species, all birds carry the same basic internal components. The development of a lightweight frame and powerful muscles has enabled them to fly.

The bill and internal organs

One of the most distinctive features of a bird is its bill. This can vary greatly in shape as well as coloration, and helps to provide valuable clues about the bird's lifestyle.

BILL SHAPES AND DIET

Members of the parrot family have a very distinctive bill structure, with the upper bill curving down over the lower bill. This arrangement enables a bird to crack seeds and nuts with relative ease. The lower bill serves as the cutting block, allowing the pointed upper bill to slice through the casing. The power in the bills of the largest parrots, such as the hyacinth macaw (*Anodorhynchus hyacinthinus*) is impressive and can reach up to 21kg per square cm (300lb per square in). Finches are also characterized by the shape of their bills, which are short and powerful, enabling them to crack seeds without difficulty.

The bill shape of birds belonging to the softbill group, however, tends to be more variable than in other groups. This reflects the fact that it is an artificial grouping, based not on shared characteristics, but on a common factor that none of these birds depends on seed as a major part of its diet. Birds that feed primarily on nectar, such as sunbirds, have long, narrow bills that enable them to probe flowers for nutrients in their native habitats. Other birds, such

The shape of a bill often reflects a bird's eating behaviour. Bills are also important for preening, and help to maintain the plumage in sleek condition. During the moult, a bird uses its bill to remove the feather casings of new feathers and to separate any loose plumage.

as starlings, have relatively pointed bills, which allow them to pluck berries (which are often swallowed whole), as well as to catch spiders, insects, and worms.

A bird's bill is made of tough keratin, a substance rather like fingernails that extends over the jaws and covers the upper and lower mandibles. If the bill of your pet bird becomes overgrown, it will need to be cut back carefully (see page 109) so that the bird can continue to eat without problems. For members of the parrot family, it is essential to provide branches in the cage for them to gnaw at to keep their bills in trim.

TONGUES

The shape of a bird's tongue varies according to species. For example, the brightly coloured bill of toucans houses a long, fringed tongue, while a finch has a flat and fairly rigid tongue. Members of the parrot family are known to use their bulbous tongues for grasping items. Parrots' tongues are also vascular, and are prone to profuse bleeding if injured. Lories and lorikeets, which have evolved to feed on pollen as part of their diet, have specially adapted tongues, the tips of which are equipped with minute projections called *papillae*. These can be raised and operate like tiny brushes, sweeping minute grains of pollen into the bird's mouth.

THE DIGESTIVE SYSTEM

Although the basic structure of the digestive tract is similar in all birds, there are a number of differences especially at the junction of the large and small intestines. These differences are often influenced by the eating habits of a particular bird group.

The crop

Birds do not have a true stomach as such, but they are equipped with a storage organ, known as the crop. Positioned at the base of the oesophagus or gullet, the crop is most evident in chicks, and carers who are hand-feeding young birds can use its relative fullness to assess whether the chicks have received enough food. Once feathers have grown over it, the crop will be less conspicuous, although the bird is still likely to fill its crop at night. If a bird has not had the opportunity to feed for a period of time, its food will bypass the crop and move directly into the next part of the digestive system. Some birds, such as doves, produce a white secretion called 'crop milk' to nourish their chicks.

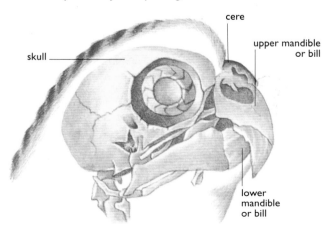

cere

upper mandible or bill

skull

lower mandible or bill

The small intestines

On leaving the gizzard, food passes into the small intestines, which consist of the duodenum and the shorter, and often narrower, ileum. The length of the intestines appears to be influenced to some extent by the bird's diet; the longest intestinal tracts tend to be found in touracos and other birds that feed on plant material. Leading from the intestines are connections to the pancreas and the gall bladder, which is embedded in the liver. Both of these assist with the digestion of nutrients, which occurs in this part of the intestines.

REMOVING WASTE MATERIAL

At the end of the large intestinal tract lies a chamber called the cloaca. This is where the urinary, alimentary, and reproductive tracts exit the body via the vent. Like mammals, birds have two kidneys, which filter blood, but they do not have a bladder for storing urine. Again, bodyweight is the prime consideration here, as a large volume of water would hinder flight and make a bird less streamlined. Instead of storing urine, therefore, birds have evolved the ability to produce a very concentrated form of nitrogenous waste, made up mainly of uric acid. This is creamy white, and is normally emptied from the body together with faeces.

THE RESPIRATORY SYSTEM

A bird's lungs are less flexible and do not expand and contract in the same way as those of a mammal, nor does air flow directly down the trachea or windpipe into the lungs. Instead, it passes through a series of thin-walled 'air sacs' that draw air through the lungs like bellows. The air sacs in some cases extend into the hollow spaces of bones, such as the humerus.

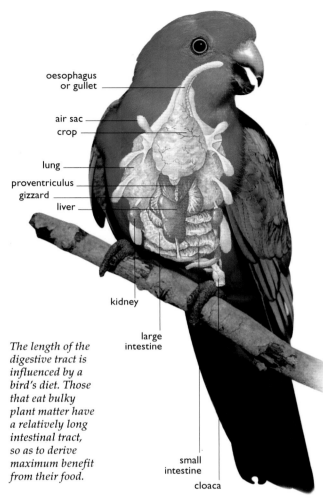

oesophagus
or gullet

air sac

crop

lung

proventriculus

gizzard

liver

kidney

large
intestine

small
intestine

cloaca

The length of the digestive tract is influenced by a bird's diet. Those that eat bulky plant matter have a relatively long intestinal tract, so as to derive maximum benefit from their food.

From the gizzard to the intestines

The process of breaking down food begins in the proventriculus, where digestive enzymes are produced. It continues in the ventriculus or gizzard, which is lined with a substance called koilin to protect against damage by the acid environment. The structure of the gizzard is dictated by a bird's diet. In nectar-feeding parrots, such as lories and lorikeets, the walls are thin, while seed-eating birds have developed much more powerful gizzards, with thickened layers of muscle that compensate for the absence of teeth to grind up food.

Seed-eating birds also include grit and gravel in their diet to help to grind the seeds in the gizzard and expose them to the digestive enzymes, so that the food can be broken down and absorbed into the body.

WARNING

When you look into a bird's mouth, the opening to the airways is located on the floor at the back. If you are passing a tube into the crop or administering liquids, you must make sure that these pass directly down the gullet into the crop. If fluid enters a bird's airways, the outcome is likely to be fatal. It is safer to have this task carried out by a vet if you are unsure. Direct crop dosing is the most effective method, because you can be certain that the bird receives the requisite dose of medication. Regular tubing for hand-feeding is not recommended because it can abrade the sensitive tissue in the neck area, which may lead to infection.

Breeding and the reproductive system

All birds reproduce by means of hard-shelled calcareous eggs. However, the number of eggs they produce in a clutch as well as the number of clutches per year varies greatly according to species, breeding conditions, and the age of the hen. If you are considering breeding your own birds, it is important to understand the process if you are to be successful.

DISTINGUISHING BREEDING PAIRS

One of the first tasks faced by bird owners intending to breed from their own birds is to recognize true pairs. If the bird species displays 'sexual dimorphism', which means that there are distinct differences between the plumage of cocks and hens, this task should be easy. The sex of an eclectus parrot (*Eclectus roratus*), for example, can be identified easily by its colour: the cock bird is a striking shade of green, whereas the hen is predominantly crimson. In fact, the difference in the plumage of the two sexes is so marked that when these birds were first discovered in New Guinea they were thought to be two different species.

In species that display no sexual dimorphism, however, sexing birds can be a problem. In such cases, it may be possible to detect behavioural differences in mature birds that are in breeding condition. Male members of the finch family, for example, have a swollen area in the cloaca called the seminal glomus, where sperm can be stored. By blowing the feathers apart to look for signs of this swelling, breeders can verify the sex of birds such as canaries during the breeding season. However, if you still find it difficult to determine the sex of your birds, the problem can now be largely overcome with the help of endoscopic (surgical) or DNA sexing (see page 72).

THE MALE REPRODUCTIVE TRACT

Cock birds have two functional testes. These are retained within the body and are located just below each kidney. The testes remain very small when a cock bird is not in breeding condition, but they increase dramatically in size during the breeding period, swelling up to 500 times larger. Most male birds do not have a copulatory organ, although ducks and other members of the Anseriformes order have a phallus. Among the Passeriformes (usually referred to as perching or songbirds), only the buffalo weaver (*Bubalornis albirostris*) has a structure developed specifically for copulation.

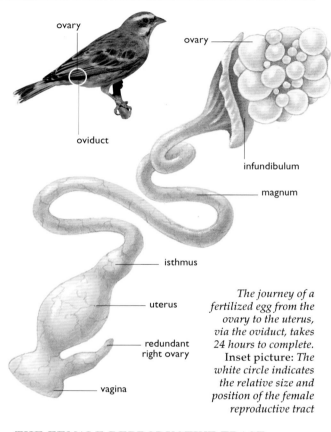

The journey of a fertilized egg from the ovary to the uterus, via the oviduct, takes 24 hours to complete. **Inset picture:** *The white circle indicates the relative size and position of the female reproductive tract*

THE FEMALE REPRODUCTIVE TRACT

The anatomy of a hen's reproductive tract is similar in all bird species. The ova, or eggs, are released from the left ovary, which is situated close to the kidney. Only the left side is functional; the right ovary and oviduct do not develop beyond the embryonic stage.

Several factors stimulate the onset of breeding condition in a hen, ranging from exposure to light (photoperiod) to the age of the individual bird. The hormone gonadotrophin is released at the onset of sexual maturity, triggering the development of the follicles in the ovary, each of which contains an ovum. These ova will be present in a hen's ovary throughout her life. When conditions are suitable, further hormonal stimulation causes some of the follicles to develop, and the area of yolk becomes clearly visible. The follicle ultimately ruptures, releasing the ovum from within, which then passes directly into the oviduct.

Fertilization

The uppermost section of the oviduct is known as the infundibulum. It is in this part of the reproductive tract that fertilization takes place, before the ovum becomes enveloped. It normally takes about a day for the ovum to complete its journey down the oviduct, from which it emerges as an egg. If, however, the ovum fails to pass into the infundibulum, it will remain trapped in the abdominal cavity. Its presence in this area of the tract is likely to give rise to a serious condition known as egg peritonitis. This causes a generalized infection and can often prove fatal. The symptoms tend to be relatively non-specific – the affected hen may simply appear to be off-colour at first. Unfortunately, this often means that the condition is not identified until the infection in the body cavity has become well-advanced. Typically, the fertilized ovum spends no more than one hour in the infundibulum, during which time the spiral bands or chalazae are added. These bands extend from the yolk and anchor it in position by attaching themselves to the opposite ends of the shell membrane.

Development of the shell membrane

From the infundibulum the ovum spends about three hours passing through the magnum, where further nutrients, including the albumen (commonly known as egg white), are secreted. Shell membranes form around the developing egg as it moves through the next portion of the oviduct called the isthmus.

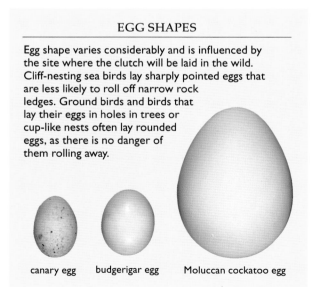

EGG SHAPES

Egg shape varies considerably and is influenced by the site where the clutch will be laid in the wild. Cliff-nesting sea birds lay sharply pointed eggs that are less likely to roll off narrow rock ledges. Ground birds and birds that lay their eggs in holes in trees or cup-like nests often lay rounded eggs, as there is no danger of them rolling away.

canary egg   budgerigar egg   Moluccan cockatoo egg

Although these membranes are not usually seen externally, they have a transparent and leathery appearance and can be seen lining the shell of an egg that has hatched.

Occasionally, a condition known as egg-binding occurs, in which the hard outer shell of an egg does not form properly. The rubbery texture of the outer membrane will be apparent when the egg is removed from the hen's body.

Formation of the shell

The shell forms around an egg in the uterus, which is also called the shell gland. The egg spends 20 hours or more in this section of the reproductive tract, even though it is a relatively short part of the oviduct. Calcium that has been carried here in the blood is used to provide the shell casing and, in some cases, colour pigments resulting from bile may also be incorporated into the egg shell.

The vagina is the last part of the oviduct, but plays no part in the development of the egg, which is fully formed when it reaches this part of the tract. There is some evidence to suggest, however, that if a bird is badly frightened just prior to egg laying, an egg may be retained here for up to several days. It may also be kept in the vagina overnight, before laying, which usually takes place in the morning. From the vagina, the egg passes into the cloaca and exits the body, pointed end first.

Egg camouflage

The colour of an egg shell is influenced by the type of nest in which the egg is to be laid. Parrots, which prefer to lay in tree hollows, generally produce eggs with white shells. This probably helps the birds to locate their clutch in the dark confines of the nest site.

In contrast, canaries construct open, cup-shaped nests that are more vulnerable to predators. Their coloured egg shells offer some protective camouflage and are often patterned with speckling, which helps to break up the outline of the egg. The colour of the shell is universal within a species, but the extent of the speckling can be highly variable.

MATING

In most birds, mating occurs as a result of semen being passed out of the male's cloaca directly into that of the female, from where it enters the oviduct. A single mating is usually sufficient to fertilize one clutch of eggs; the sperm is able to survive for at least one week in the female's reproductive tract.

Incubation, growth, and hatching

The number of eggs that a bird lays is influenced by the age of the hen. Generally, birds laying for the first time and old birds tend to produce smaller clutches than average. Nutrition may also be a factor in determining clutch size, although birds with poor eating habits are unlikely to breed at all.

THE INCUBATION PERIOD

Once a fertile egg has been laid, it needs to undergo a period of incubation, during which the embryo can develop and ultimately emerge as a chick. Although the incubation periods given for individual bird species are generally reliable, discrepancies may arise with the first eggs of a clutch. This occurs because incubation does not necessarily take place from the moment when the first eggs are laid. Sometimes, a hen may not start sitting in earnest until she has produced the majority of eggs in her clutch, thus prolonging the anticipated hatching date by several days. The effect of this delay in incubation is that the chicks emerge over a shorter period of time so there will be less discrepancy in their sizes. This should in turn help to ensure that a higher percentage of the offspring is reared successfully. This is particularly significant in birds breeding in the wild.

Fertile eggs remain viable for up to a week or so, provided that incubation has not begun. However, a sharp drop in temperature causing the eggs to be chilled after this point could be fatal for the embryo.

EGGS: CANDLING AND HYGIENE

You should keep egg-handling to a minimum, especially in the early stages of incubation. Although the yolk is held fast by bands of thick albumen, jolts can be fatal, so it is best to use a technique known as candling to keep a check on the fertility and development of eggs (see page 76). This used to involve holding the egg in front of a lighted candle to illuminate the blood vessels, which would confirm that it was fertile. Today, you can buy special candling lights, which produce the same effect as a candle flame and can be used without the egg being picked up – a much safer process.

Bacteria and other harmful microbes can easily be transferred from your hands to an egg via the microscopic pores over the surface of a shell. To avoid infecting and killing the developing embryo, adopt these basic rules of hygiene into your handling routine.

- Use soap-based products containing antibacterial agents to wash your hands before handling eggs.
- Avoid contaminating your hands again immediately after washing them by drying them on a towel – use disposable paper towels.
- Dry your hands thoroughly, because an egg is more likely to slide through wet fingers.
- Always wash your hands between handling eggs from different nests to prevent the risk of any cross-contamination.

Phases of development

Immediately after hatching, the chick (here, a budgerigar) is featherless and blind. It rests with its head hanging down.

— eyes closed

nestling down

eyes open

At 13 days, the chick is covered in nestling down and the wing feathers are visible. Its movements are still quite uncoordinated.

At about 20 days, the head, back, and wing feathers are coloured.

coloured feathers appear

flight feathers still undeveloped

At 26 days, the colour of the adult plumage is fully established. Pied budgerigars retain the coloured and white or yellow areas throughout life.

The frequency with which eggs are laid varies according to the type of bird: parrots tend to lay on alternate days, whereas finches and softbills generally produce their eggs on consecutive days until the clutch is complete.

Double-clutching

The onset of incubation normally ends the cycle of egg-laying. However, if the first clutch of eggs is taken away from the hen just after she has completed laying she is likely to start producing a second clutch. This phenomenon has formed the basis of double-clutching, a technique that has been used successfully by breeders of large parrots, in particular, to increase the reproductive potential of their birds.

The first clutch of eggs is then incubated artificially, and the resulting chicks raised by hand, leaving the adult pair to hatch and care for their second round of offspring without any interference. Double-clutching has proved very valuable with breeders of this group of birds, because parrots have a long breeding cycle, which can extend for four or more months.

Incubation duty

Incubation is often the sole responsibility of the hen bird, although breeding pairs of cockatiels (*Nymphicus hollandicus*) and most pigeons and doves share this duty. Breeders of some species, such as canaries and hummingbirds, put the cock bird with the hen during the mating period only and then remove him so that he does not interfere with her nesting activities.

When the chick is 32–35 days old, it is fully fledged and able to fend for itself outside the nest. By this stage, the flight feathers and tail are clearly apparent, while the dark markings visible on the upper beak soon fade.

flight feathers

tail feathers developed

Development inside the egg

Within the fertilized egg, chick growth begins in the germ cell, a white area that is evident on the yolk. A delicate array of blood vessels spreads out over the yolk, at the centre of which the embryo forms. At regular intervals throughout the incubation period, a sitting bird will turn the egg to prevent the growing chick from becoming stuck to the membrane of the inner shell. This is also essential for eggs that are being incubated artificially.

The pores in the shell provide the necessary air for the chick to breathe as it grows within the egg and its oxygen requirement rises accordingly. The outer chorion and allantois, which are membranes from the gut, fuse together and spread, forming a network of blood vessels (the chorio-allantoic membrane) that lines the inside of the shell. Acting rather like a passive lung, oxygen from outside the shell diffuses into the blood vessels via the pores, while carbon dioxide passes in the opposite direction out of the shell.

As the embryo grows, the yolk decreases in size. The shell gradually becomes thinner, from which the developing bird absorbs calcium into its body, and a gap known as the air space starts to form at the blunt end of the shell. The chick normally becomes orientated so that its neck adjoins this part of the egg, with its tail pointing down towards the sharp end.

HATCHING OUT

A build-up of carbon dioxide in the shell triggers 'internal pipping', which marks the first stage of hatching. About 48 hours before the egg is due to hatch open, the chick's head breaks through into the air space. This enables it to start breathing air directly for the first time rather than relying on the network of blood vessels. If the embryo is in the wrong position within the shell, it is likely to require a vet's assistance if the hatching process is to be completed successfully.

At the same time, the chorio-allantoic membrane starts to dry up in order to reduce the amount of blood lost when the chick finally hatches. To cut its way out of the shell, the chick uses its egg tooth. This temporary structure is located close to the tip of the upper bill and which is shed soon after hatching.

Most chicks are helpless and blind at birth, with only traces of down feathers on their bodies. Their subsequent development may then be very rapid: budgerigars are ready to leave the nest after one month, while young finches may take flight even earlier, usually within two weeks of hatching.

Bird senses

Of all the senses, eyesight is the one that birds rely on most heavily for detecting predators and escaping from danger. This is confirmed by the large size of their eyes relative to the size of the skull. The senses of smell and taste are not as well developed in birds, compared with mammals, but their sense of hearing is acute.

EYES AND SIGHT

Although not immediately obvious, the visible part of a bird's eye is comprised of two parts; the pupil is the black disc at the centre through which light enters the eye; the iris is the coloured outer ring that surrounds the pupil. In birds, as the iris is often very dark or blackish, it tends to be indistinguishable from the pupil.

Using iris colour to age and sex birds

The colour of the iris often changes throughout a bird's life and is a useful guide to the age of an individual bird. For example, as a chick, the African grey parrot (Psittacus erithacus) has very dark almost black irises, which become grey, and then turn bright yellow at about 12 months. The pale straw-yellow

In many birds, such as Bourke's parakeet (Neophema bourkii), the iris is so dark that it is barely distinguishable from the black pupil at the centre of the eye. Relatively large eyes reveal that a bird is more active at dusk than at mid-day.

coloration in the irises of mature individuals emerges from about five years onwards. It is also possible to use the coloration of the iris to distinguish between the sexes of cockatoos belonging to the genus *Cacatua*. Most noticeable in a good light, the irises of mature cock birds are usually black, but reddish-brown in hens. This feature is especially apparent in lesser sulphur-crested cockatoos (Cacatua sulphurea).

Varying the diameter of the pupils

Unlike mammals, birds are able to vary the diameter of their pupils independently of the prevailing lighting conditions. This is most apparent in male members of the parrot family, which constrict their pupils as part of their display ritual making their eyes appear momentarily more colourful (see page 20).

Red eyes

In the case of some colour mutations, such as the lutino (see page 36), the absence of melanin from the plumage extends to the eyes, making them appear red. This is caused by the blood supply at the back of the retina and does not appear to impair the bird's eyesight.

The surrounds of the eye

The modified feathers on a bird's eyelids have an identical function to eyelashes, preventing debris from entering the eyes and causing inflammation.

The area of bare skin around the eyes is more prominent in certain birds than others. In diamond doves (Geopelia cuneata), this skin provides a way of distinguishing between the sexes, as it is more prominent in the cock birds, especially during the breeding season. Any abnormal swellings found in the skin around the eyes might be an indication of an underlying respiratory infection. If the bird's sinus becomes swollen, it will press on this area and distort the skin.

NOSTRILS AND SMELL

Although birds possess an olfactory system for smelling and tasting, research suggests that they do not utilize it to any significant extent. In most birds the nostrils are located above the upper bill, with the exception of kiwis (Apteryx spp.), whose nasal openings are visible at the tip of their long bill. This enables them to detect worms and other food by smell.

Recognizing nasal problems

The shape of the nostrils varies between different bird groups. When examining a bird, it is, however, important to check that both nostrils are the same size. If one appears to be enlarged, it could be an indication that the bird is suffering from a long-standing respiratory infection that may flare up in the future, particularly when the bird is moved to a new environment. Grey parrots are especially susceptible to this type of problem so always check adult birds for symptoms.

Nasal plug

While checking a bird, you may notice a plug of material in one or both nostrils. This plug represents a past discharge that has hardened and dried and is abnormal. While vets can treat the underlying cause (which is often linked in part to a deficiency in vitamin A), the damage to the nasal opening will be permanent.

TASTE

Birds have a limited sense of taste compared with that of mammals. Scientific studies, however, have revealed several differences in the way that birds react to different tastes. Hummingbirds and some parrots, which feed on flower nectar in the wild, discriminate positively when offered sugar solutions, whereas no such reaction occurs in the case of starlings or siskins.

Taste buds

The taste buds are often located not on the tongue, but in the surrounding area of the mouth and on the palate in the roof of the mouth, which has a bony structure in all birds. Parrots have only about 350 taste buds in their mouths, compared with 9,000 taste buds in humans. The distribution, however, is related to the passage of food through the mouth prior to swallowing, since birds do not chew their food, but tend to swallow it directly.

Taste development in chicks

Taste buds seem to be especially important in chicks, helping them to recognize what is edible in the post-fledging period. This is the time when a bird's feeding preferences are developing. From this stage onwards, a young parrot will readily eat a complete diet, yet an adult bird that has been reared on a regular diet of sunflower seed is less easily persuaded to adapt its feeding preferences, in spite of being offered a more nutritious and balanced alternative.

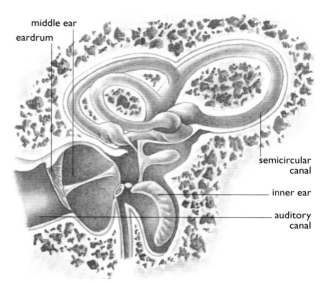

middle ear
eardrum
semicircular canal
inner ear
auditory canal

Sounds are channelled into the ear via the auditory canal, causing the eardrum, a tight membrane between the outer and middle ear, to vibrate. These vibrations are then carried through the middle ear to the inner ear, so they can be sensed.

EARS AND HEARING

Birds have an acute sense of hearing, in spite of the fact that their ears are concealed beneath the feathers on the sides of their faces. Brushing these back gently will reveal the openings here – there are no ear flaps.

Like a human ear, a bird's ear is divided into the outer and middle ear, which are linked by the auditory canal. There is a difference, however, in that sounds hitting the tympanic membrane, or eardrum, in one ear also reverberate through to the membrane of the other ear as well, hitting its inner surface. This is thought to help small birds to locate the direction of sounds, which could be crucial. The three semicircular canals in the middle ear also help the bird's sense of balance. The primary hearing range in which birds can detect sounds lies between 1–5kHz, with an upper hearing limit of approximately 10kHz. Like humans, birds can distinguish sounds between these frequencies; this is perhaps not surprising because bird song is a complex form of vocalization, like speech itself.

Ear problems

Macaws often suffer a congenital problem involving the membrane that covers the entrance to the ear canal. If the membrane has not opened up by the time the bird is five weeks old, the skin has to be perforated by a vet to establish full hearing.

Sociability, aggression, and pair-bonding

Birds are sociable creatures. Many wild birds, especially those that live in open countryside, form large flocks, which has the important advantage of there being many more eyes and ears to detect the approach of possible danger. Some parrots such as sulphur-crested cockatoos *(Cacatua galerita)*, appoint individual birds to act as sentinels when the rest of the flock is feeding. Their task is to concentrate exclusively on looking for any hint of danger, crying out to warn the others. Within seconds of one bird detecting danger, the whole flock wheels away to safety.

SOCIABILITY AND THE AVIARY

This instinctive sociability is so entrenched in some birds that breeding results in an aviary can be adversely affected unless several birds of the same species are housed within sight and sound of each

Parrots of different species may form flocks together, like these macaws and pionus parrots gathered at a mineral lick in Peru.

other. Incredible as it may seem, after being bred and domesticated over the course of more than 150 years, one of the main reasons for a single pair of pet budgerigars refusing to breed is because they are isolated from other budgerigars. The introduction of a second pair of birds invariably resolves the problem, and both pairs will proceed to nest without hesitation.

Aviary in-fighting

When keeping birds in an aviary, it is important to understand that an established flock is a stable community that does not welcome newcomers readily, particularly during the breeding period. If you bring a new bird into an existing collection, severe fighting may result. Should you intend to breed budgerigars as a group in an aviary, wait until you have all the pairs together before releasing them into a flight equipped with a good selection of nest boxes, and avoid introducing any new birds until the breeding season is over (see page 67).

Peach-faced lovebirds (*Agapornis roseicollis*) can be particularly spiteful even outside the breeding period and are often kept in individual pairs, although some breeders have managed to maintain them with great success in colonies. It is a good idea to have more than a couple of pairs in your collection, so as to reduce aggression between particular individuals.

Aggression towards young birds

Young birds may interfere with a second round of eggs being laid or suffer an attack by the cock bird and should therefore be removed once they are known to be feeding independently. Outbreaks of aggression towards fledged young are especially common among Australian parakeets such as the grass parakeets (*Neophema* spp.), although budgerigars and cockatiels are surprisingly tolerant of their offspring. *Forpus* parrotlets and other prolific members of the parrot family are most likely to be spiteful towards their fledged youngsters. This reflects the desire of the cock bird to breed again, and male offspring tend to be at greatest risk of being attacked.

INFLUENCE OF NATIVE HABITATS

Large parrots such as macaws often stay together as a family group in their native habitat, until the next breeding season. Unlike the prolific parakeets from Australia, these birds are slow to mature and produce relatively few offspring – rarely more than two in a season – and even mature pairs do not necessarily breed every year. These larger parrots invest considerable time in rearing and caring for their chicks, guiding them through the early months when mortality is likely to be higher. To some extent, this lifestyle reflects the stable environment in which they occur, whereas Australian parakeets face a much harsher landscape, where the ability to take advantage of favourable conditions and breed rapidly can be an important factor in the survival of the species.

Sociability of finches

Finches, which have a relatively short lifespan of no more than one or two years in the wild, can also be prolific in aviary surroundings. You may find it helpful to have more than one couple of finches of the same species for breeding, even if you are keeping a mixed collection. This should help to ensure that you have at least one true pair, in cases where it is not possible to sex these birds visually, and also allows them to form a small flock, which encourages their breeding instincts.

PARROTS AND HUMANS

Psittaculid parakeets rarely develop into tame and confiding companions, unlike grey parrots which naturally form very strong pair bonds. The bird readily transfers this affection to its owner and so establishes a close relationship with the person caring for it.

One important point to remember when you introduce a parrot into your household, however, is to involve other members of the family in caring for the bird. If your parrot is allowed to identify solely with you, the bird could become aggressive towards any one else who tries to approach it.

PAIR-BONDING

Within flocks, pairs will form, especially during the breeding season. Birds with a short lifespan, such as finches tend to form loose bonds, and it is common for cock canaries to mate readily with several hens in succession. Among the softbills, however, longer-lived species, such as hornbills, which have a life expectancy of several decades commonly pair-bond.

Choosing breeding pairs

Among the parrots, while budgerigars and many other parakeets are fickle in their choice of partners, larger parrot species pair for life. For this reason, when buying large parrots, it is advisable to look for a true breeding pair that has already produced offspring, because there is no guarantee that a single cock and hen, especially mature birds, will prove to be compatible. A bird farm where several birds are housed together might increase your chance of finding an established pair. Look for birds that remain together when resting and follow each other closely around their quarters.

Should one of an existing pair die, it may be possible to introduce another partner successfully, although an element of luck is needed. The birds are unlikely to develop an instant rapport, but look for signs of mutual preening and feeding, as these are indications that the pair may bond. The ideal, but expensive, way to obtain a compatible pair is to buy four or six birds and allow them to select their own partners.

Psittaculid parakeets such as Alexandrine (*Psittacula eupatria*) and plum-headed (*P. cyanocephala*) parakeets do not pair-bond throughout the year. Outside the breeding season, hens are spiteful to cock birds, but become more amenable at nesting time. Avoid pairing an older hen with a young cock, since he is likely to remain timorous, reducing the possibility of mating.

Understanding bird behaviour

The way in which a bird behaves can provide valuable insights into understanding your pet. In some cases, it may even help to prevent you from being bitten! Many owners of parrots, in particular, do not realize that these birds rely heavily on body language for communication.

Hand-reared chicks often behave like their aviary-bred or wild counterparts, indicating that these traits are instinctive. For example, after weaning a young parrot will continue to solicit feeding by hand by bobbing its head, seeking reassurance from its owner, in the same way as it would from a parent bird.

BEHAVIOURAL TRAITS IN PARROTS

A recognizably threatening gesture in parrots is when one bird stalks slowly and deliberately along a perch towards another, holding its head low and its bill open. The other bird is likely to respond by opening its bill, standing up on the leg nearest to the aggressor to emphasize its height, and then moving away, often flying to another perch.

Wing displays

Parrots often use their wings to display aggression. For this reason, the leading edge of the wing is usually brightly coloured. Even in species with predominantly green plumage, such as Hahn's macaw *(Ara nobilis)*, the leading edges of the wings are bright red. When the bird is at rest, this red feathering is usually kept concealed, but when the parrot rises to challenge a rival member of the flock, its wings are held slightly away from the sides of its body, bringing the red plumage into view. Should a stronger deterrent be needed, the parrot may actually open out one of its wings more fully and strike at its opponent. This action is usually sufficient to make the rival retreat; however, if the challenge is continued, the aggressor may use its bill, although it will rarely inflict a painful bite. It is probably not entirely coincidental that the bills of psittaculid parakeets and other parrots are often red.

Tail-flaring

Tail-flaring is performed as a threatening gesture by lovebirds and *Poicephalus* parrots when they have established a nest site and want to warn other birds away from their territory. Similar behaviour is also apparent in the broadtail group of Australian parakeets, such as the rosellas *(Platycercus* spp.), which are popular aviary birds. In most parakeets, the tail feathers taper down to a tip, but in rosellas they have a constant width and can be flared out as a warning gesture and waved back and forth, reflecting a bird's agitated state.

Bill-sparring

A milder form of aggressive contact seen in yellow-collared macaws *(Ara auricollis)* is bill-sparring, whereby two birds fence with their bills, until one of them finally backs off. This activity often seems to be a type of game rather than a hostile encounter, and is usually accompanied by high-pitched, rather excitable calls. It may also be a way used by birds to reinforce the existing hierarchy within a group.

Courtship disputes

White cockatoos *(Cacatua* spp.) are sensitive birds and among the most highly strung of the parrots. For this reason, they need careful management, especially if you are intending to breed them. As they approach breeding condition, these cockatoos, like many parrots, become more destructive and noisy than usual. The cock bird displays to his intended mate, throwing his crest feathers forward in a gesture to attract her attention. Should the hen not accept his advances, he is likely to launch a ferocious attack on her, leaving her seriously injured or dead. The risk of this problem is highest in hand-reared birds that have not been bred together before, and the temperament of a tame male cockatoo can change markedly even at this stage.

Courtship feeding

Body language generally assumes greater importance during the breeding period. The most obvious sign in parrots is likely to be constriction of the pupils (see page 16), which may lead to the cock engaging in courtship feeding of the hen, prior to mating. Cock

---

WARNING

It is not unusual for cockatoos to feign attention and then reward the outstretched hand with a painful bite. Among the worst offenders are Moluccan *(Cacatua moluccensis)* and lesser sulphur-crested *(C. sulphurea)* cockatoos. Such birds cannot be recommended as companions for a home with young children, because of the uncertain temperament of adult birds.

Cock birds can often be seen feeding their reflection in mirrors. This behaviour usually indicates that the bird is in breeding condition, as it views the reflection as a partner.

budgerigars that are kept on their own maintain this behaviour, and will feed their reflection in a mirror. This habit can become harmful to the bird if it persists over a period of time (see pages 108–9) and you may need to remove the mirror from the cage.

BEHAVIOURAL TRAITS IN FINCHES

Before they start nest-building in earnest, male finches often collect a sprig of nesting material that they proffer to their intended mates as an initial gesture. This sprig is likely to form part of their courtship dance, which entails raising and lowering the head and is often linked with song.

Bill pecking

At this stage in the courtship cycle of some birds, such as waxbills, bill-pecking is common. One member of the pair prods its closed bill at the tip of the other bird's bill. When she is ready to mate, the hen leans forward on the perch with her tail slightly quivering up and down. This behaviour may also be seen in other bird groups, including softbills, and in almost every case, except for members of the crow family, the hen vibrates her wings gently as well as her tail.

MUTUAL PREENING

Even when living in flocks, birds reinforce the pair-bond by mutual preening. Such behaviour, whereby one member of the pair gently preens the back of the neck of its partner, is very common in a wide range of species, from small finches to large macaws. It is also the reason why a tame parrot often ruffles the feathers on the nape of its neck and sits with its head forward to encourage its owner to stroke its plumage.

MODIFYING A BIRD'S BEHAVIOUR

Not all of the behavioural patterns that you might observe in a tame pet bird will be seen in an aviary, as parrots can be encouraged to act in different ways. At its most extreme form, this can be seen in birds that are taught to ride small bicycles, usually for paid performances. Clearly this does not mimic any natural behaviour. It is also alien for birds to lie on their backs, with their wings closed and feet in the air, although parrots can be taught to rest in this way from an early age, and do so readily, without obvious distress. This reflects a degree of trust in their owner, because the birds are exceedingly vulnerable in this position, being unable to fly away immediately if threatened.

Birds that can talk

The arrangement of a bird's vocal apparatus is significantly different from that of mammals. Instead of having vocal chords, which vibrate to produce sound, birds rely on a structure known as the syrinx, located close to or at the point where the windpipe divides into the two bronchi, entering the lungs. Muscles and cartilage are involved in producing the sound, which is amplified via a resonating chamber, known as the tympanum.

TALKING PARROTS

Parrots are, without doubt, the most talented talking birds, yet out of 330 species of parrot, relatively few are able to amass large vocabularies. Young parrots appear to acquire part of their vocabulary from mimicking their parents. In particular, grey parrots rank as one of the most popular pets because of their ability to acquire human speech – some birds even have discernible local dialects in the wild.

How much does a parrot understand?

The fact that a bird can repeat words does not mean, of course, that it actually understands what it is saying. Many bird owners are convinced that their pets have a grasp of what they are saying, but the bird may simply be responding to what has been said to it, rather than understanding the words it has spoken.

Purchasing a parrot that can already talk

Parrots are exceptionally long-lived birds and have good memories. This can be a drawback if you buy a parrot that is already talking, because you may find it difficult to discourage the bird from saying unsuitable words that it may have acquired in its vocabulary. You may be able to condition the bird to clean up its language by placing a cover over its quarters and plunging it into darkness for a few minutes whenever the offending words are uttered. By attempting to teach the parrot different words, there is also the hope that the earlier words will fade from its memory (see pages 70–1). However frustrating it may be to revise the bird's vocabulary or teach it new words, you must never punish a parrot physically in any way. This is likely to cause irreversible damage to your relationship with your pet, as well as being cruel and unnecessary. Parrots do not forget mistreatment and often react badly, screeching loudly in fear when approached by the person who has inflicted the punishment.

Why parrots screech

Although parrots talk in a voice that is conversational in tone, they can also screech loudly if frightened or excited. Unfortunately, this can be a drawback to keeping large parrots in urban areas, where their calls might aggravate your neighbours. This applies especially to Amazons, which screech regularly in the early morning and again at dusk, when they would be leaving or returning to their roosting sites. Very little can be done to curtail this instinctive behaviour, other than designing an aviary shelter that will restrict the sound of the birds and placing their nest box inside, so that they can be shut in overnight. They will soon become used to the routine, which also gives them added security from cats or foxes at night.

If you acquire a tame adult bird that starts to screech for no obvious reason when you approach, it may be that you are wearing a particular colour that reminds the bird of a distressing episode in its past.

Fashionable young ladies in the 19th century often kept talking birds as pets.

MYNAHS

Like parrots, hill mynahs possess impressive talking skills and can become equally tame. They are superb mimics, too, not just of words but also of household sounds – it can be very difficult to tell the difference between a doorbell being rung and a mynah imitating the sound. Sadly, it is almost impossible to persuade the bird to lose a sound from its repertoire.

Purchasing a mynah

Mynahs are members of the starling family. If you are looking for one as a pet, it is important to start with a young bird. These are easy to identify because they do not have the prominent wattles (the fleshy yellow areas of skin at the back of the head) associated with adult hill mynahs. Young birds have a duller appearance and lack the glossy iridescence that is most prominent around the adult's neck. Young mynahs are often described as 'gapers' because of their habit of begging for food with open mouths.

MIMICRY IN OTHER BIRDS

Besides the mynah, other starlings, including the common starling (*Sturnus vulgaris*) and even some members of the crow family, have been known to talk, especially when reared by hand. Another softbill, the shama (*Copsychus malabaricus*), has one of the most melodic songs in the entire bird kingdom. There is no record of this bird repeating speech, but if a cock shama is housed within earshot of other birds, it will incorporate the call of these birds into its song.

It has also been known for zebra finch chicks (*Poephila guttata*) reared in isolation by Bengalese finches (*Lonchura domestica*) to replicate the exact song of their foster parents. Even when they are returned

The greater hill mynah holds the record for mastering one of the longest words in the English language - antidisestablishmentarianism.

to a flock of zebra finches, such birds continue to sing like Bengalese finches, confirming that imprinting occurs at an early stage of the bird's development.

Canaries may occasionally recite a few words, but they are much more responsive to sounds that can be used to form the basis of their song pattern. They are traditionally taught to mimic the sounds of mountain streams in the Harz Mountains in Germany, where they evolved, using 'schoolmaster' birds and audio cassettes.

RESEARCH INTO THE SPEECH ABILITY OF BIRDS

The parrot's ability to talk has become a subject for serious investigation by scientists over recent years, thanks mainly to Dr Irene Pepperberg and her grey parrot called Alex.

Based within the Department of Biological Sciences at Purdue University in the United States, Dr Pepperberg sought to discover Alex's ability to reason, derived from the words that he learned, rather than the words themselves. Alex soon came to distinguish between different objects, asking for those that he needed and rejecting those that did not match up to his request. This power of recognition and especially the bird's use of the negative, revealed a clear ability to understand what he was actually saying.

Alex was successfully taught the concept of colour, to the extent that he asked to identify his own colour, and soon added the word 'grey' to his vocabulary. Unlike many pet birds, Alex was deliberately not taught directly as this approach can lead to a passive reaction, with the parrot simply repeating what it hears, rather than taking an active part. Alex was conditioned to express himself by watching and learning from two people, much in the same way that a young parrot in a flock would acquire knowledge from watching older members of the group.

The development of bird-keeping

The first birds to be kept by humans were working birds such as hawks, which were trained to catch game for the table. In China, cormorants would be tethered to a boat to catch fish. A loop fitted around the bird's neck prevented it from swallowing the fish it had caught under water.

BIRD-KEEPING IN ANCIENT TIMES

The first real evidence of birds being kept as pets dates back to about 1500BC in ancient Egypt where they are known to have been displayed in Queen Hatshepsut's menagerie. China, too, has a long tradition of breeding birds, and is the original home of the popular Bengalese or society finch (*Lonchura domestica*). These birds are domesticated hybrids and probably result from crossing the white-backed mannikin (*Lonchura striata*) with other eastern *Lonchura* species. Songbirds and ornamental pheasants have also long been highly prized in China.

The Classical world

An interest in parrots was kindled in ancient Greece by the returning armies of Alexander the Great, which brought back psittaculid parakeets, notably the Indian ringneck (*Psittacula krameri*) and the species now known as the Alexandrine parakeet. One of the great fascinations of these birds was their apparent ability to converse in several languages. In fact, they were simply reciting sounds and, compared with other species of parrot, had a very limited repertoire. The Romans fell under the spell of parrots too, housing them in special cages of rare and precious materials. Ringnecked parakeets maintained their popularity as pets during this period, and it is possible that the Romans were the first to encounter grey parrots.

Roman aviaries

The remains of aviaries using netting or metal bars to contain the birds have been unearthed at various Roman sites and are mentioned in contemporary accounts. One of the most magnificent structures from this era was constructed for Terentius Varro at Casinum, where both songbirds and parrots were housed. Only wealthy citizens could afford to keep a collection of exotic birds, while less affluent people kept a variety of native birds, such as talking magpies, which were common attractions in barbers' shops.

INTO EUROPE

Birds from islands off the coast of Asia first became known in Europe during the reign of King Frederick II (1198–1250) of Sicily, who later became Holy Roman Emperor. His aviary, known as the Vivarium, housed a variety of birds, including an umbrella cockatoo (*Cacatua alba*) given to him by the Sultan of Babylon. Under Frederick's patronage, birds were studied at close quarters for the first time but, unfortunately, most of the drawings and texts based on his observations have not survived.

Throughout the Middle Ages birds, such as pigeons, were kept increasingly as a source of food, particularly at monasteries.

Wealthy Roman families had slaves whose sole task was to care for and train the household's pet bird.

Dovecotes were often set up on a large scale, and although the early timber buildings have disappeared several later stone structures have survived in Britain.

Birds from the New World

Elsewhere in Europe, voyages of discovery started to introduce parrots from the New World. Christopher Columbus returned from the Americas with a pair of Cuban Amazon parrots (*Amazona leucocephala*) in 1493. After being displayed in a triumphal parade through the streets of Barcelona, the birds were cared for by his patron, Queen Isabella of Spain.

Before long, it became highly fashionable to collect birds from far-off countries, and other parrots including macaws were brought back for the crowned heads of Europe. In England, Henry VIII's grey parrot was renowned for hailing boats across the River Thames at Hampton Court and then demanding that the boatmen be paid for their journey! The famous Bird Cage Walk through St James's Park in London takes it name from the display of birds organized there by Charles II. His favourite bird was a crane that had been given a replacement wooden leg, following an injury.

Housing for ornamental birds began to figure prominently in the design of stately homes and palaces during the 1700s. Catherine the Great of Russia had aviaries at many of her palaces, while the Bird House in Knowle, Kent, built in 1761, was equipped with fireplaces, allowing 23 exotic species of bird to be kept successfully through even the coldest English winter.

THE RISE OF THE FANCY

Canaries were already well established as popular pet birds in Europe by the 18th century, and the start of the Victorian period saw the development of the modern canary fancy, that is, breeds developed for their ornamental qualities. Canary clubs started to become popular in Britain during the 1840s, each holding regular meetings and observing a set of rules. Support for the clubs was strongest in coal-mining areas where canaries were used to warn workers of a shortage of oxygen in the mine shafts. Miners took the birds underground in cages and watched them carefully for any signs of breathing distress that would indicate that it was no longer safe to remain in that part of the mine.

Several of today's popular type-breeds owe their existence to the local mining communities in areas such as Yorkshire. Sadly, not all the breeds from this period have survived, although the Old Varieties Canary Association has successfully recreated the Lancashire and encouraged the continued breeding of others.

Naturalists eagerly studied the new and exotic species of bird introduced to Europe by explorers of the New World.

Budgerigars

While the working classes remained loyal to the canary, bird-keeping in the latter part of the Victorian era became dominated by budgerigars, which appealed primarily to the rising middle classes. A large industry was spawned as a result of the popularity of the budgerigar, with fashionable shopping catalogues offering exotic designs of bird cages and aviaries. Although the price of budgerigars fell dramatically once breeding became widespread, the appearance of new colours maintained the huge level of interest in these birds for more than a century.

Only recently has the popularity of budgerigars declined as a result of increased competition from other birds. Today, growing numbers of hand-reared parrots are available, thanks to improved techniques that make it possible to reliably sex species in which there is no difference in plumage between cocks and hens. For the first time, the budgerigar faces serious rivalry from other members of the parrot family, notably the development of many colour varieties in Australian parakeets, as well as the cockatiel and peach-faced lovebirds.

The effects of domestication

Domestication has had a marked effect on bird species kept today. In its native habitat, an unusually coloured individual would be vulnerable to predators, and even if it did survive to breed successfully, there would be little prospect of its features being reproduced in any offspring. In captivity, however, birds can be paired in accordance with the rules of inheritance (see pages 92–3), making it possible to nurture new colour forms and hopefully ensure their successful development.

Today, selective breeding to replicate distinctive characteristics, such as a certain colour plumage, unusual feathers, singing ability, or size means that modern bird-keepers are presented with a vast choice.

DOMESTICATION OF THE CANARY

A good example of how domestication can alter the appearance of a wild bird species is the canary, which has been domesticated longer than any other pet or

The four categories of modern canary bred today can trace their origins back to their ancestors in the Canary Islands, but many years of domestication mean that they are now quite distinctive from green wild canaries.

aviary bird. Modern pet canaries bear little resemblance to their wild ancestors on the Canary Islands, which local farmers started to breed for export as early as the 1550s. Thankfully, the breeding process in birds has not resulted in the widespread physical weaknesses often encountered with dog breeds. The different forms of canary, described as breeds, have developed into four categories: singing, type, posture, and new colour.

Singing canaries

Singing canaries, such as the American singer and related breeds, are kept primarily for their song rather than appearance. They tend to be relatively small in size, with a finch-like body shape.

Type canaries

Greater divergence has resulted in the so-called type canaries, which are bred and judged on the basis of their appearance. Distinguishing features are very important, even though some birds have been developed from a variety of other breeds, including Norwich, Belgian, and Lancashire stock.

A new breed can only be considered to be established when it has achieved a uniformity in appearance, which will take a number of years. Even when it has finally become established though, a breed will continue to evolve in line with changes to the exhibition standard. For example, today's Yorkshire fancy canaries are much broader at the shoulder than their Victorian ancestors, and they are also much taller.

Many canary breeds remain localized with only a few attaining an international following, which explains the diversity in their appearance. Frilled canaries are, for example, popular in continental Europe, ranging from the North Dutch frill through the Parisian and Swiss frills to the *gibber italicus* and *gibboso espagnole* of southern Europe, but none has ever achieved a strong following in Britain or North America.

Posture canaries

Not only do posture canaries need to excel in type and condition during judging, but they must also be able to adopt a characteristic posture. This trained ability accounts for up to 50 per cent of the points awarded to a bird. Not surprisingly, few posture breeds remain, possibly because showing them is demanding. The best known posture breed is the Belgian fancy, which has had a large impact on the development of other breeds, such as the Yorkshire fancy and the Scotch fancy, which is assessed in part for its movement in front of the judge, known as 'travelling'.

New colour canaries

This category includes red-factor canaries, which result from early genetic experiments carried out in the 1920s. The aim was to create a red canary breed, by crossings with a South American finch, known as the red-hooded siskin *(Carduelis cucullata)*. This did not prove possible, as the young cock birds emerged with a coppery tone, and the hybrid hens were grey, like the hen siskin. Breeders continued to refine these birds, mating the best-coloured hybrids and siskins to improve the depth of red coloration as far as possible. This laid the foundations for today's red-factor canaries, but it is now clear that their coloration depends to some extent on diet, such that colour feeding during the moult (see page 94) is vital for these birds.

Natural colour mutations have also occurred in the canary fancy. This has formed a distinctive group, of particular appeal to fanciers interested in genetics.

CROSS-BREEDING AND MULING

While the offspring from crossings with red-hooded siskins are fertile, cross-breeding canaries with other finches has been popular for even longer, even though their offspring very rarely reproduce. The technique described as muling is simply a particular form of hybridization – the mating of two different species, producing hybrid offspring. Mules bred from crossing cock canaries and native finches have proved popular at exhibition for many years. The offspring combine the attributes of both parents: goldfinch mules are colourful and sing well, while linnet mules are less attractive but are said to be the best songsters of all mules.

BUDGERIGARS

Domestication of budgerigars has produced many thousands of colours and combinations. While emphasis has been placed on type and colour for exhibition, the actual structure of the feathers has been affected too, albeit less obviously. As with canaries, this has given rise to buff birds, with coarser plumage than their yellow counterparts (see pages 32–3).

Variations in budgerigar plumage

Accepted plumage variants in the budgerigar are restricted to three crested variants: a full circular crest; a half-circular crest; and tufted forms. Those variants not encouraged in breeding programmes include

Goldfinch mules, the offspring of cock canaries and hen goldfinches, retain the attractive coloration of goldfinches, with the melodic singing ability of the canaries.

long-flighted birds, in which the flight feathers of each wing cross over the lower back. Although it may seem that colour variants in budgerigars have been exhausted, breeders are still hoping to achieve a black specimen. Genetically, this is a viable possibility, unlike suggestions of a pink budgerigar, which is genetically impossible. The emergence of the spangle mutation (see page 37) has already had a marked effect on exhibition studs worldwide, while the development of clear-bodied budgerigars is evidence that other exciting possibilities still appear from time to time.

COLOUR MUTATIONS IN OTHER BIRDS

As the domestication of other species has occurred, so colour mutations have also emerged. The speed with which these can be established depends largely on the age of maturity in an individual species. Lovebirds and cockatiels, for example, can be bred when they are about 12 months old, whereas ringnecked parakeets are unlikely to nest successfully before they are three years old. This makes it a longer and potentially more hazardous process to establish mutations in these parakeets, especially at first when there may be only a single individual with the desired coloration.

Colour mutations of large parrots are still scarce at present, although blue and lutino Amazons of various species are occasionally being bred in small numbers. Genetic changes are not always the sole cause of a change in colour, however, particularly in birds where only a few feathers are affected. The more likely source of colour mutation in these cases is a metabolic disorder, stress, or diet (see page 94).

Group profiles

Before choosing your bird, you need to be clear in your mind whether you are looking to keep an individual bird as a pet and companion, to build up an aviary of mixed birds, to make a specialist collection of one type of bird, or even to breed, groom, and train birds for competitive exhibitions and shows.

Introduction to bird groups

There are three groups of bird – finches, softbills, and parrots – that suit being kept as caged or aviary birds. Within each group is a variety of species, with its own distinctive coloration, feathering, and habits. Such is the scope offered by bird-keeping that it is important to identify where your interest lies at the outset, if for no other reason than you need to plan the right accommodation for your bird and equip it with the necessary basics. If you change your mind at a late stage and opt for a different aspect of bird-keeping, you are likely to encounter further costs. For example, an aviary designed for finches is unlikely to suit large parrots, whose destructive nature demands a more robust structure. When looking for a pet bird, you should also bear in mind the expected lifespan of a species; budgerigars often have brief lives of about 6 years, whereas cockatiels can live for 18 years.

The hardiness of a species is an important factor when assessing the type of accommodation needed for your bird. Some small birds, such as tropical finches and the smaller softbills, may not be hardy enough to survive outdoors in winter without additional heating in their housing. In such cases, you need to decide whether to house them in a specially equipped bird room in wintertime or to bring them indoors. You may also need to compensate for reduced daylight in winter by providing additional heat (see page 52). If small tropical birds are faced with, perhaps, less than eight hours of daylight in which to feed, they may become vulnerable to hypothermia.

If you intend to exhibit your birds, a bird room is essential, together with breeding cages, to house individual pairs, and special show cages. Raising a stud of exhibition birds to competition standard takes up a lot of time but can be very rewarding (see page 71).

KEY TO SYMBOLS

◓	pet bird	▲▲▲	5	typical clutch size (number of eggs)
🐦	aviary bird			
◙	closed nest	🥣	18	typical incubation period (in days)
⊔	open nest	🐦	14	typical fledging period (in days)

FINCHES AND CANARIES

Members of the finch family, which also includes canaries, are primarily seed eaters. Lively and colourful, they can be housed in large flight cages, but breeding is more likely to be successful within a planted flight. In cool climates, they may need extra heating in winter. Some finches are popular as exhibition birds.

Star finch

The song of cock canaries has ensured their popularity as pets, but these birds can also be housed in a mixed aviary and are available in a wide range of colours from pure white to dark green. These and other domesticated finches can be bred in cages. Turn to pages 30–3 for more further information on finches and canaries.

Green singing finch

SOFTBILLS

This category somewhat artificially groups together a vast range of birds of very different sizes and habits, according to their usual diet of soft foods.

Bearded

Although different species vary, softbills generally feed on fruit, nectar, and insects, as well as special softbill foods and pellets. Many species of bird qualify for inclusion in this group, however the better known and easiest to keep are the starlings, toucans, tanagers, babblers, white-eyes, barbets, and sunbirds.

Due partly to their messy eating habits, most softbills are kept as aviary birds, with the exception of the greater hill mynah, which is a talented mimic and often kept in the home as a pet. Many of the softbill group are frequent bathers and need the

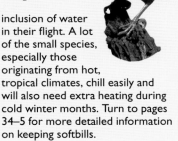

Sclater's orange-headed tanager

inclusion of water in their flight. A lot of the small species, especially those originating from hot, tropical climates, chill easily and will also need extra heating during cold winter months. Turn to pages 34–5 for more detailed information on keeping softbills.

PARROTS

The extremely popular parrot family includes budgerigars, cockatiels, lovebirds, small parrots, parakeets, and the large parrots. The group feeds mainly on seeds, nuts, fruits, and greenstuff. Lories and lorikeets feed on nectar. Turn to pages 36–47 for more detailed information on keeping members of the parrot family.

Orange-winged Amazon

• **Budgerigars** Widely kept as companions and popular as aviary and exhibition birds, budgerigars are available in a wide range of varieties and colours, from the pure snow-white albino through to violets.
• **Cockatiels** Available in a wide range of colours, cockatiels can learn to talk and whistle well and are ideal as indoor pets, or aviary birds.
• **Lovebirds** Bred in a wide range of colours, lovebirds, especially if hand-reared, make delightful pets, and also thrive in a garden aviary. They tend to be less raucous than other parrots and may learn to repeat a few words.
• **Small parrots** Some of the smaller parrots, such as the *Forpus* parrotlets, and poicephalid and hanging parrots, are well suited to a garden aviary.
• **Parakeets** This group, which includes rosellas, is ideal for aviaries, often nesting readily in such surroundings, but they may be too nervous to become good pets.
• **Large parrots** The large parrots, many of which have a similar lifespan to humans, include macaws, Amazon parrots, pionus parrots, African greys, and cockatoos.

Stanley or western rosella

Young, hand-reared parrots can develop into superb pets, and are talented and amusing mimics However, these magnificent birds are by far the most expensive to buy and house in aviaries. If you are considering keeping parrots in an aviary, you need to be aware that their loud calls can become a cause for complaint from neighbours, and handling these birds, especially untamed adults, can be difficult for inexperienced handlers, as they can inflict painful bites.

Finches

A wide range of finches is kept and bred in aviary collections. Although Old World species predominate, Australian finches, such as Gouldian and zebra finches, are now well domesticated, with colour variants becoming increasingly common.

BENGALESE FINCH

 5  15  21

Since its introduction to Europe and North America, the domesticated Bengalese finch (*Lonchura domestica*) has become popular as an exhibition bird. These birds are also known as society finches, being widely used as foster parents for hatching and rearing the young of other finches that prove less reliable when breeding.

AFRICAN WAXBILLS

 5 12 21

African waxbills are so called because their reddish bills supposedly resemble red sealing wax. Sexing of waxbills outside the breeding season can be difficult, but the cock of the widely kept red-eared waxbill (*Estrilda troglodytes*) and the similarly coloured St Helena waxbill (*E. astrild*) can be distinguished during the breeding period by the stronger pinkish hue of its abdomen. In another popular species, the orange-cheeked waxbill (*E. melpoda*), hens may be recognized by their slightly paler cheek colour. All African waxbills tend to be rather nervous and do not appreciate being disturbed when nesting.

Waxbills sometimes construct a domed nest with a false 'cock' nest above the chamber in which the chicks are reared. This design may deter nest predators, who are confronted with an apparently empty nest. In a planted aviary, you need to provide closed nesting boxes where a pair can build their nest if they prefer.

Most *Estrilda* species cannot be sexed visually but they tend to be social birds and breed readily when kept in small groups of the same species. A nest box placed high up in the aviary may encourage breeding. They are reliant on live food throughout the rearing period.

Waxbills will benefit from being provided with a probiotic and electrolyte (see page 67) when you bring them home. Remember that these birds prefer warm, sunny conditions so do not transfer them to an outdoor aviary too early in spring.

MUNIAS

 5 12 21

Also known as mannikins, munias are estrildids from Asia and Africa. They are slightly larger than African waxbills, averaging 10cm (4in), and their colouring is more subdued, with shades of brown and black, often broken by white markings. Munias breed more successfully because, unlike African waxbills, they do not rely on live food in the rearing period. Sexing munias visually is impossible, but you can stimulate breeding by housing them in groups and providing nest boxes. Once acclimatized, the birds tend to be hardy, although they may need heating and lighting in winter.

Bengalese finches have become popular exhibition birds, particularly as a range of colours have been developed, ranging from white, through chocolate, to fawn. This is a chocolate-and-white colour variant.

Pairs of blue waxbills, such as the red-cheeked cordon bleu (Uraeginthus bengalus) *can be housed with* Estrilda *species but may prove aggressive to their own kind.*

only the male
of this species
has red cheeks

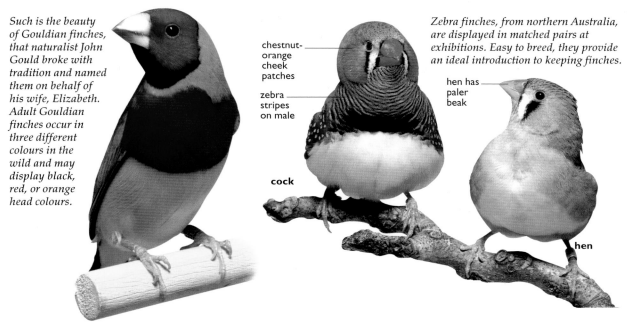

Such is the beauty of Gouldian finches, that naturalist John Gould broke with tradition and named them on behalf of his wife, Elizabeth. Adult Gouldian finches occur in three different colours in the wild and may display black, red, or orange head colours.

chestnut-orange cheek patches

zebra stripes on male

cock

Zebra finches, from northern Australia, are displayed in matched pairs at exhibitions. Easy to breed, they provide an ideal introduction to keeping finches.

hen has paler beak

hen

GOULDIAN FINCH

 5 14 21

Gouldian finches (*Chloebia gouldiae*) naturally have red, black, or orange heads; the young have much duller nest feathers. Mutations have included white- and blue-breasted forms, in different head colours.

Gouldian finches are relatively demanding to look after, especially during the weaning process which should not be rushed. They need indoor heated accommodation when kept in temperate climates, and are usually bred in warm surroundings in breeding cages as they often nest in cold months. When choosing Gouldian finches, select stock that has been bred naturally rather than fostered under Bengalese finches, as they are more likely to nest successfully on their own once mature.

These finches are prone to an infestation of air-sac mites (see page 106), which can be detected by a bird wheezing or resting with its bill slightly open.

SINGING FINCHES

 5 15 21

The green singing finch (*Serinus mozambicus*) and its grey relative (*S. leucopygius*) are talented songsters, that may live to be 20. Cock birds sing through much of the year, except during the moult. Although these birds are related to the canary, their song is not as varied or rich.

WEAVERS AND WHYDAHS

 3 14 15

When in full colour, weavers and whydahs are often described as 'IFC' to distinguish them from birds that are out of colour (OOC). The cock birds keep harems of several hens and their plumage changes dramatically at the start of the breeding season. For example, the orange bishop (*Euplectes orix*) develops a stunning orange ruff, with orange feathers down its back and glossy black body plumage. Male whydahs develop magnificent trailing tail plumes to impress their mates, which may lay their eggs in the nests of waxbills rather than incubating them. Both weavers and whydahs are relatively hardy once acclimatized.

ZEBRA FINCH

 5 12 19

The zebra finch (*Poephila guttata*) takes its name from the black and white stripes on the cock bird's chest, although a wide range of colour variants has been developed, including the well-established cream, silver, and fawn varieties, a pied mutation, the recent orange-breasted and black-breasted forms, and a crested form. Hens can usually be recognized by the paler reddish shade of their bills. An ideal introduction to bird-keeping, these birds are easy to breed in a cage or aviary using nesting baskets or boxes.

Canaries

The development of the canary fancy has led to the creation of several sub-groups and even at a typical show, you are unlikely to see all categories represented. Those kept primarily for their singing prowess, such as the roller, are not usually displayed at the same events as type, posture, and new colour canaries, so as to maintain the quality of their song. Correct lighting is also a major concern to those organizing shows for new colour birds in particular, because anything other than natural daylight can create an undesirable yellowing of the canaries' appearance.

STARTING TO KEEP CANARIES

If you are interested in breeding a specific branch of the canary fancy, as distinct from keeping a single cock bird as a pet, or in an aviary, then you need to seek out breeders who can offer you quality stock. Remember to start looking for breeding pairs in early spring, well in advance of the breeding season, as supplies of quality stock quickly become exhausted at this time of year.

To help you establish a clear idea of what you want to achieve with your birds, it is a good idea to join a specialist society for the breed that appeals to you, and visit shows regularly to see which canaries enjoy the most success. It is also important to be aware of the rules about show cages and the colour feeding of birds during the moult (see pages 74–5), because not all breeds are permitted to have their colour modified in this way.

BUFF AND YELLOW FEATHER TYPES

You should be able to identify whether a canary is a buff- or yellow-feathered bird from a close examination of its plumage. Buff birds tend to have coarse feathers, and the colour pigment does not extend right to the edges, which makes the plumage appear slightly paler than that of yellow-feathered birds. It is more difficult to see this difference in white canaries, although yellow-feathered specimens usually have a sleeker appearance than buff-feathered birds, and are more tightly feathered. Conversely, distinguishing between the two feather types is easiest in red-factor canaries, where buffs have a frosted appearance, especially in the neck plumage where the feathers are small and plentiful. Breeders often describe these birds as 'apricot', and refer to yellow-feathered specimens as 'non-frosted' or 'red-orange'.

COLOUR VARIATIONS

Several technical terms that are used by canary fanciers may be applied either specifically to a particular variety or generally for all breeds. These criteria are important, because they determine which class your bird should enter at shows. Wrongly classed entries are disqualified, so if you are not sure which class to select, ask an experienced fancier for advice.

Variegated canaries • These have only broken areas of dark melanin plumage. Heavily variegated indicates a dominance of melanin, while lightly variegated indicates that paler areas predominate.

Gloster canaries (here, a buff corona Gloster) occur in both crested (corona) and non-crested (consort) forms. All crested canaries currently have flat rather than tufted crests.

When breeding crested canaries, always pair crested and non-crested individuals, such as this green consort Gloster together, and never two crested birds. This maximizes the likelihood of crested chicks being produced.

Border canaries (here, a variegated yellow border) are often referred to as 'wee gems'.

Self canaries • A uniform dark colour, such as green.

Clear canaries • No melanin pigment in the feathers, which typically appear pure yellow or white.

Foul • A dark-coloured canary with a small area of paler feathers.

Ticked • A light-coloured canary with a small area of darker feathers.

Lizard canaries

The lizard canary is the oldest surviving breed and ranks among the most distinctive, because of its pattern of lizard-like markings. Buff-feathered birds are described as silver, and yellow-feathered individuals are referred to as gold. The clear area of plumage often present on the head is described as the cap, of which there are three variants: the clear cap; the broken cap, where the area is split by darker markings; and the non-cap, which has no trace of clear feathering.

Plumage of young birds

The term 'unflighted' describes young birds that have moulted for the first time, although at this stage they shed only their body plumage. As a result, in colour-fed birds the flight feathers will be paler than the new plumage, since without a blood supply they cannot absorb the colouring agent. Only when the plumage is fully replaced, at one year, does the coloration become consistent, and the bird is described as 'flighted'.

BREEDING CANARIES

Canaries rear two broods of chicks during the spring and summer, before moulting. As soon as your canaries start to display signs of breeding behaviour, with cocks singing loudly and hens seeking nesting material, put out nest pans for the birds to use as the basis of their nests. Stitch special felt linings in place through the

The rich depth of colour of this red-factor canary comes from its breeding and from judicious use of a special colouring agent, which is provided during the moulting period. The new colour canaries are prized for their coloration.

holes in the bottom of the nest pan to provide a soft lining. It is best to provide nesting material that is sold solely for this purpose, as some alternatives may be harmful to the birds. Introduce the material in small amounts, adding more only when the hen has used up the first supply. If you put out too much material, it is likely to end up on the floor and quickly become soiled.

Mating and egg-laying

It is quite usual for a cock canary to be mated with two or more hens, so you may find it useful to have a double or triple breeding cage with removable partitions. Separate the pair once egg-laying has started, and carefully remove the eggs, replacing them with dummy eggs up until the morning of the fourth day when the final egg of the clutch is due to be laid. Place the eggs in a container lined with cotton wool and store them in a cool place until the clutch is complete. They should then be put back in the nest and the dummy eggs removed. This results in all of the chicks hatching on the same day, and being the same size gives them an equal chance of survival.

If you want your hen to lay again, provide her with a clean nest pan and reintroduce the cock bird once the first round of chicks has been moved to separate accommodation.

A suitable rearing food should be offered to the hen and chicks throughout the rearing period. Young canaries leave the nest by the time they are about 14 days old. They are likely to show a preference for soft food rather than hard seed when they become independent after about three weeks.

WARNING

Feather cysts or 'lumps' sometimes arise over a bird's wings. They are caused by feathers that curl back towards the follicle, where debris gradually builds up. The cyst has a cheese-like appearance and protrudes through the surrounding plumage. Eventually, it may drop off or it can be removed surgically. Recurrences are common and are thought to result from repeated pairings of birds with the soft buff feathers preferred by breeders. To eliminate cysts, avoid breeding affected individuals with other canaries, although they can be used safely for crossings with finches to yield mules.

Softbills

Some softbills can be demanding, but the species described here are relatively easy to keep. They can be housed in outdoor aviaries in the warmer months in temperate areas, but some, particularly smaller species, need additional heating and lighting in wintertime.

STARLINGS

 2–5 🪺 14–8 🐦 20–8

Purple glossy starlings *(Lamprotornis purpureus)* tolerate other non-aggressive birds of similar size, but pairs are best housed on their own. Bathing facilities are essential for glossy starlings to keep their plumage in top condition. They use a nest box in the breeding season, which they line with small twigs and other material. Newly hatched chicks need to be fed on live food, so offer adequate supplies until the young leave the nest.

Other closely related starlings include the identically sized green glossy starling *(L. chalybaeus)*, which is metallic green in colour, and the long-tailed glossy starling *(L. caudatus)*, with iridescent green and blue plumage. Perches for these birds need to be sited carefully to prevent tail feathers from rubbing against aviary mesh. Once glossy starlings are acclimatized, they may be overwintered outdoors in temperate areas, but must be shielded from bad weather (see page 55).

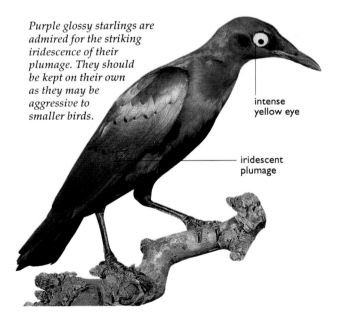

Purple glossy starlings are admired for the striking iridescence of their plumage. They should be kept on their own as they may be aggressive to smaller birds.

intense yellow eye

iridescent plumage

wing colours show when resting

Pekin robins are the most colourful members of the babbler group and have an attractive song. In an aviary they can become quite tame.

Starlings from northern Asia are hardier than their African cousins and vary in coloration. The Chinese starling *(Sturnus chinensis)* is sexually dimorphic, and has an attractive soft shade of grey, broken by white and black areas of plumage.

Mynahs

The pagoda starling or mynah *(S. pagodarum)* has orangish-brown plumage, with darker wings and a black crown. Like other starlings, this species has immaculate feathering and proves to be alert and inquisitive by nature. You can tame this bird quite easily in aviaries, with offerings of live food.

Best-known as a pet bird, the greater hill mynah *(Gracula religiosa)* is a talented mimic and makes a lively aviary bird. It often breeds successfully in captivity. Mynahs are messy eaters, and their perches need to be cleared of debris regularly to avoid foot infections.

BABBLERS

 4 🪺 14 🐦 14

Belonging to a group of birds known as babblers, one of the most popular softbills is the Pekin robin *(Leiothrix lutea)*, which is neither a robin nor exclusively of Chinese origin. These birds are very easy to keep, eating invertebrates, fruits, and even seeds. Although they can be housed with birds of a similar size, they have a reputation for stealing eggs during the breeding season. To encourage a pair of Pekin robins to breed, create a planted area in your aviary with bamboo.

Another of the babblers, the silver-eared mesia *(L. argentauris)* is similar in size to the Pekin robin and has mostly orange plumage, a predominantly black head, and silvery ear patches. Although these birds are quite hardy, they need snug winter quarters, with heating available in very cold weather. Another member of this group of babblers is the blue-winged siva *(Minla cyanouroptera)*, with bluish coloration predominating in its plumage. Cocks in particular have an attractive song.

WHITE-EYE OR ZOSTEROPS

With more than 80 species of white-eye or zosterops and many more subspecies, it is difficult to distinguish certain birds. One of the easiest to recognize is the chestnut-flanked zosterops *(Zosterops erythropleura)*, because of the chestnut markings evident along the sides of its body. Nectar should always be available for these birds, and fruit and small invertebrates should be given regularly. Remember to include plenty of small live food in their diet once the chicks have hatched.

Although white-eyes can be housed outside in planted aviaries during the summer in temperate areas, they need heated accommodation throughout winter. Nesting pairs build small cup-shaped nests, often using moss and gossamer from spiders' webs. Like many softbills, these small birds are avid bathers, so provide a shallow dish of clean water daily for this purpose.

TOURACOS

Hartlaub's touraco *(Tauraco hartlaubi)* and the white-cheeked touraco *(T. leucotis)* are among the most commonly kept species of touraco. Other popular

Zosterops, like this Indian white-eye, are often considered pests in their native countries where they damage fruit crops.

crest

white cheek

Touracos (here, a white-cheeked touraco), have a broad bill to enable them to pluck berries. They can also open their bills wide so as to swallow fruits whole.

species are the violaceous touraco *(Musophaga violacea)*, a large bird with distinctly violet plumage, and the grey go-away bird *(Crinifer concolor)*, named after its call.

Touracos are large birds that need to be housed in a spacious aviary. They have flexible perching grips, enabled by their ability to move their rear toes, but their feet are also quite delicate and vulnerable to frostbite in winter. Some touracos are reluctant to eat loose softbill food, but ensure that they have a balanced diet by mixing pellets in with diced vegetables and fruit.

When the male touraco comes into breeding condition before the hen, it may be aggressive towards her. Make sure that there is enough plant cover where she can hide or, if the cock is persistent, you may need to clip one of his wings. This phase passes once egg-laying commences. Nesting pairs build platforms of twigs, and will use a secluded wooden shelf.

OTHER SOFTBILLS

Barbets have strong, powerful bills and tend to be aggressive. They occur in the New World as well as parts of Africa and Asia. Tanagers are exclusively confined to the Americas. The most popular species are the colourful *Tangara* tanagers which cannot be sexed visually. Both tanagers and barbets are at risk from iron storage disease, and so should be offered low-iron diets (see page 87).

Budgerigars

albino
cock

lutino
cock

Albinos are the result of a total absence of both yellow pigment and melanin, while in lutinos only melanin pigment is absent.

The budgerigar is a unique member of the parrot family. Its scientific name *Melopsittacus undulatus* derives from the Greek *melos* meaning 'song' and *psittakos* meaning 'parrot', while *undulatus* is Latin and means 'wavy-lined', referring to the patterning that extends from the head to the wings. The small violet cheek patches have three black spots beneath them.

COLOUR VARIANTS

The light-green coloration associated with the native form of the budgerigar is still quite common among the many different colour varieties bred today. Like most parrots, budgerigars may have two colour pigments present in their feathers: a yellow pigment and a dark pigment known as melanin. Budgerigars are broadly divided into blue-series and green-series groupings.

Blue and green series

Although blue budgerigars are common, there is no blue pigment as such, and the blue colour is achieved by the structure of the plumage. The 'blue layer' is sandwiched between the outer part of the feather containing yellow pigment and the inner core where melanin is located. It reflects back light, creating the impression of blue. In areas where the blue layer is overlaid by yellow, with melanin behind, the plumage appears green, in the same way that mixing blue and yellow paints produces green. The melanin has a key role, since it effectively activates the blue layer. Where melanin is absent, the plumage will be yellow. Where the yellow pigment is absent, the plumage will be blue.

Dark factor

Within each category of green and blue, there are now different recognized shades, thanks to the emergence of the 'dark factor'. This was first recorded in France in 1915, but is one of the very few mutations known to have occurred at an earlier stage in the wild. There may be one or two dark factors present, with the possibilities as set out in the following table.

DARK FACTORS		
	Green series	Blue series
No dark factor	Light green	Sky blue
One dark factor	Dark green	Cobalt
Two dark factors	Olive	Mauve

Other colour varieties

Visual violet • This is a separate mutation from blue, produced when the violet factor combines with mauve.

Lutino • This is a stunning mutation in which rich buttercup-yellow plumage arises from a total absence of melanin. This particular mutation is a sex-linked recessive (see page 82), an important consideration when pairing birds, to maximize the likely number of lutino offspring in a nest.

Albino • These pure white birds with red eyes arise when both yellow and melanin pigments are absent. Under certain lighting an albino may have a faint bluish tinge to its plumage, because the blue layer is still present.

MARKINGS AND CRESTS

The appearance of pied budgerigars opened many new possibilities for breeders. There are two types:

Australian dominant pied • The body markings of this fairly large

Only one dominant pied parent (here, a pied dark green budgerigar) is needed to produce pied offspring.

budgerigar are random, with variable proportions of clear and coloured areas. Any shade of green can be linked with yellow, while combinations of blue and white also occur. The eyes are dark and the iris ring is visible in mature birds.

Danish recessive pied • These small birds are easily recognized by their plum-coloured eyes. The pied characteristic is a recessive feature, so breeding is more difficult. While repeated pied-to-pied matings produce all-pied offspring, outcrosses to normal birds are important to increase size, even though pied chicks from such pairings will not appear until the second generation (see pages 82–3).

Crested • There are three crested mutations: full-circular, half-circular, and tufted. Good crests are difficult to breed. Never pair crested budgerigars together.

This grey crested budgerigar has a full circular crest.

This opaline grey budgerigar has a clear 'V' at the top of its wings.

Opaline • These budgerigars have muted, dark wavy patterning on their heads. Prize specimens display a clear V-shaped area at the top of the wings. Reduced melanin may produce undesirable random dark markings, known as 'flecking', on the forehead.

Yellow-faced blue • It is unusual to see white and yellow feathers on the same budgerigar, but they may occur, producing a body plumage in a separate colour from the face.

Spangle • In well-marked birds of this recent variant, the throat spots are reversed as is the typical patterning, so that dark markings are confined to the edges of the feathers on the back and wings. Clear visual differences exist between single- and double-factor birds (see pages 82–3), with the markings of the latter being most impressive.

The visual violet mutation combines the violet factor with mauve.

BREEDING

Budgerigars should not be allowed to rear more than two rounds of chicks in succession. If you are breeding a colony in a garden aviary, provide twice as many nest boxes as pairs and fix them at the same height around the aviary, to avoid the risk of fighting between hens.They do not need nesting material.

Just before laying starts, the hen's droppings become larger and have a pungent odour. The hen sits alone, although the cock may join her for short periods. Once the chicks have hatched, the concave of the nest box soon becomes soiled and needs changing regularly. Scrub it clean and allow it to dry before returning it to the nest. Be meticulous about hygiene if any pairs have French moult (see page 102), as you may spread the infection from one group of chicks to another. Nest dirt can accumulate on the underside of the chicks' upper bills or on their tongues and may cause malformation. Carefully remove it, using a blunt-ended cocktail stick. Clean soiled claws by softening the dirt in tepid water and then breaking it away.

WING COLOURS

Changes to wing colour has produced yellow-wings and white-wings, in which the dark markings of green- and blue-series birds have become diluted. Grey-wings retain darker barring on their heads and wings, while in cinnamons, the melanin pigment is modified to a brownish tone. Where a bird's markings are modified, it is standard practice to give this description first: for example, an opaline white-wing sky blue.

Cockatiels

The cockatiel (*Nymphicus hollandicus*) has long been overshadowed by the budgerigar, but the wide range of colour variants being developed has seen its popularity grow among pet owners, breeders, and exhibitors. Cockatiels often live to the age of 18 or beyond, have melodic voices and a talent for mimicry, and are not destructive by nature.

COLOUR MUTATIONS

The colour range in cockatiels is limited, as their feather structure lacks the blue layer present in budgerigars. Grey predominates in their natural plumage, varying from light shades through to almost black – mature cock birds display the darkest plumage.

Pearl

The scalloped appearance of pearl mutations varies according to the extent of the markings and the number of feathers affected. The mutation causes a dilution of melanin in the centre of feathers, which is usually most evident over the back and wings. Where the affected areas are elongated, the bird is sometimes described as a lacewing. In most strains of the pearl mutation, these pale areas are lost as the cock bird matures, being replaced by normal feathers. However, a few pale feathers may remain around the shoulder.

Lutino

Lutino cockatiels are one of the most widely kept mutations of this species. Their lemon colour varies in depth; birds displaying the more desirable, deeper shade are described as buttercups.

WARNING

A widespread problem common to lutino cockatiels is the habit adults have of feather-plucking their chicks, which is, unfortunately, incurable. Once the chicks have left the nest, their plumage regrows, but until new feathers are produced, these birds are more vulnerable to chilling during cold weather and may need to be brought indoors.

Another problem that is often seen in certain strains of lutino cockatiel is a lack of feathering behind the crest. Where this occurs, the area remains bald and plumage never emerges. Try to avoid affected birds, especially when selecting breeding stock.

6–7   19   35

The lutino cockatiel was developed by a Florida breeder called Mrs Moon, which led to such birds first being known as 'Moonbeams'. The lutino is the most popular colour form of cockatiel.

lemon colour

young birds have shorter tails

yellow face

A native of Australia, the cockatiel was first seen in Europe during the 1840s and, like the budgerigar, was soon breeding freely in collection. In grey cockatiels (shown here), the cock bird has distinctive yellow face patches.

crest can be raised and lowered

cock

hen

White-faced

White-faced mutations result from the lack of yellow pigment in the bird's plumage – there is no yellow coloration on the faces of cock birds and hens have predominantly grey heads. The orange cheek patches are absent in both sexes.

Pied

The pied characteristic can occur in combination with any colour of cockatiel, except the albino. The markings can vary widely between individuals, and if the hen lacks pigmentation, it sometimes makes sexing on the basis of tail and head coloration unreliable.

Cinnamon

Cinnamon mutations, sometimes described as isabelles, have distinctly brownish tinges to their plumage, which also extend to the legs, feet, and eyes. The depth of coloration varies between individuals, with cocks tending to display the darkest shades.

Dominant silver

Since it first appeared in 1979, breeders have been able to increase the numbers of these attractive silver birds comparatively rapidly, as it is a dominant mutation. Unusually, it is possible to distinguish visually between the single- and double-factor forms (see pages 82–3) of the dominant silver: single-factor birds are darker than their double-factor counterparts. It has also proved possible to combine silver and white-faced mutations to create the white-faced dominant silver, which is more commonly known as the platinum.

Pied cockatiels (shown here) have highly individual markings but these are not always produced in the offspring.

pied marking

It is possible to combine the characteristics of a cinnamon cockatiel (shown here) with a pied mutation to create cinnamon pieds, which have areas of cinnamon feathering offset against pale lemon patches of plumage.

cock

NEW COLOURS

Considerable scope now exists for breeding cockatiels that combine up to four separate mutations, such as white-faced pearl cinnamon pieds. The pure-white albino cockatiel is, in effect, a white-faced lutino, and so devoid of any pigmentation.

Other recent mutations include the yellow-face and the pastel-face, whose coloration is visible in the cheek patches. These two mutations raise the prospect of darker plumage in future mutations, which may result in an orange-faced cockatiel. Cockatiels are attracting considerable interest from breeders, and the different colours are being standardized for show purposes.

BREEDING

Cockatiels are gentle birds and can safely be housed in a mixed collection, even alongside small finches such as waxbills. They are unusual among parrots in that the incubation duties are shared between the cock bird, who sits during the day, and the hen who takes over this duty at night.

Unfortunately early mortality can be high among newly hatched chicks, and is often caused by a *Candida* infection (see page 105). This is present in the adults and rarely causes symptoms in them, but it is lethal to their offspring. If a *Candida* infection is confirmed, then it is important to review the birds' diet, as a deficiency of vitamin A may be implicated. Correcting this deficiency helps to ensure that the chicks are reared without problems in the future.

Lovebirds

There are nine different species of these popular small short-tailed African parrots, although one of these, Swindern's black-collared lovebird (*Agapornis swinderniana*) is rarely kept. The remaining eight species can be broadly divided into two groups: the white eye-ring group and the sexually dimorphic group.

WHITE EYE-RING GROUP

Members of the white eye-ring group of lovebirds can be identified by the ring of bare white skin around their eyes. Although none of the four species in the group can be sexed visually, breeders often rely on signs of preening between two birds to recognize pairs.

You may be able to breed these lovebirds in a colony system as long as the group is well established before you put in the next boxes. Provide a good choice of boxes at the same height to minimize the risk of fighting. The four different species are:

Masked lovebird (*A. personata*) • This is the most colourful member of this group, and is recognizable by the broad yellow area of feathering on the chest extending around the neck. Different colour varieties include the dilute form known as the yellow-masked and the blue-masked, descended from a wild individual, which when combined ultimately produce the white-masked, a paler variant.

Fischer's lovebirds (*A. fischeri*) • The brightly coloured Fischer's lovebirds make attractive aviary occupants,

and nest quite readily, building relatively bulky domed nests within a nest box. Provide plenty of fresh twigs for them at nesting time so they can strip the bark and use it as a lining. The first recorded colour mutation in this species was a blue form, which appeared in aviaries in South Africa during the 1950s. Unfortunately, hybridization involving blue masked lovebirds has meant that a number of supposed blue Fischer's lovebirds are actually impure stock. This applies to some of the other colours now in existence – hybrids in this case are fertile, reflecting the very close relationship between all four members of the white eye-ring group.

Nyasa lovebirds (*A. lilianae*) • Probably a more common sight in Australian than in European collections, Nyasa lovebirds can prove to be prolific in the right surroundings. They are less aggressive than related species, and can be housed in colonies, which seems to improve breeding success. These birds need heated quarters in temperate areas during the winter, as they are not fully hardy.

Black-cheeked lovebird (*A. nigrigenis*) • This lovebird is the smallest member of the group. A genuine blue mutation, rather than one from crossings with blue-masked lovebirds, was recorded in Denmark in 1981. The resulting birds are larger in size and have no pearl marking at the base of the bill. A true yellow variant is also currently being developed in Denmark.

white eye-ring

Abyssinian lovebirds are the largest of the sexually dimorphic group of lovebirds.

The best way of visually sexing masked lovebirds is to watch their behaviour. The hens alone usually carry the nesting material.

hen

cock

Hand-reared peach-faced lovebirds make delightful pets and may even learn to repeat a few words.

The pastel blue peach-faced lovebird was first bred in Holland in 1963. It is now popular worldwide.

PEACH-FACED LOVEBIRDS

Peach-faced lovebirds (*A. roseicollis*) share various characteristics with members of the white eye-ring group but lack the obvious feature. They are quite hardy but always provide them with a nest box for roosting, as they tend to be susceptible to frostbite. In all other respects, these birds are robust and can sometimes be aggressive, particularly during the breeding period. Peach-faced hens are responsible for building the nests, carrying strips of material in among their feathers rather than their bills. When first hatched, the chicks are covered in a coat of red down. Two popular colour forms of this bird are:

Pastel blue peach-faced • One of the most widely kept colours is the pastel blue, in which the absence of yellow pigment produces a greenish hue. The facial area is pale salmon pink, rather than pure white as seen in genuine blue mutations. The lutino, with its brilliant yellow plumage offset against a reddish face, also has red eyes and pinkish feet.

Pied peach-faced • The pied mutation in the peach-faced is widely seen in association with colours such as the normal and pastel-blue forms. The dark factor is equally well established, with both dark green (single dark factor) and olive (double dark factor) variants, as in the budgerigar. Grey, fallow, and cinnamon colours are all established, but probably the most exciting development of recent years has been the breeding of violet peach-faced birds, where the light blue of the lower back and rump is transformed into a striking visual violet. Attempts have also been made to hybridize peach-faced specimens with other lovebirds, but the resulting young have proved infertile.

This attractive cremino variety results when lutino and pastel-blue mutations are combined.

SEXUALLY DIMORPHIC GROUP

This group of lovebirds comprises the following species:

Red-faced lovebirds (*A. pullaria*) • With the exception of the stunning lutino variant, colour varieties are unknown in red-faced lovebirds, which are named after their characteristic red facial plumage. These birds are less hardy than other species, and need constant heat during the winter months in temperate areas. Sadly, they are not easy to breed, as the hens do not sit tightly on their clutch, causing the eggs to chill. In their native habitat, red-faced lovebirds nest in termite mounds, where the heat within the chamber keeps the eggs warm. You might achieve successful breeding results, however, by placing a thermostatically controlled heat pad inside the nest box, set at a temperature of 30°C (85°F).

Madagascar lovebird (*A. cana*) • This species is easier to breed, although pairs tend to nest in winter when indoor heated accommodation is needed. Some nervous pairs are easily disturbed. Look out for breathing difficulties, which might be caused by an infestation of air-sac mites (see page 106).

Abyssinian lovebird (*A. taranta*) • This is the largest member of the lovebird family, and is fully hardy. Pairs of Abyssinians need to be housed separately, and use relatively little nesting material. You may notice hens plucking some of their breast feathers to make a soft lining in the nest box, but there is no need to be alarmed as these feathers grow back again in due course.

Small parrots

Many of the smaller parrots are ideal for a garden aviary, being quiet by nature and not too destructive. Although there is no strict division between small parrots and parakeets, the two should not be confused. It is generally accepted that parrots have short, square tails whereas those of parakeets are distinctly longer.

CELESTIAL PARROTLETS

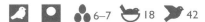 6–7 18 42

Celestial parrotlets *(Forpus coelestis)* are now available in an increasing number of colour variations, of which the blues are the most common. They can usually be sexed visually, as hens have green plumage whereas cocks are more brightly coloured with distinct blue markings. Although they rank among the smallest parrots, celestial parrotlets are highly aggressive and should be housed in individual pairs, unless you can provide very large quarters. Where the birds are kept in adjoining flights, use wire to divide the panel on both sides to stop them from attacking each other's feet.

Use budgerigar nest boxes for nesting birds, but instead of a concave, line the floor with shavings sold as animal bedding as these are dust-free and non-toxic. Many pairs of parrotlets are prolific and are likely to rear two broods in rapid succession. Keep a watchful eye when banding the chicks, as adult birds often try to remove the rings in the nest and may cripple their offspring in the process.

POICEPHALID PARROTS

 4 28 84

The poicephalid parrots originate in Africa, where nine species can be found. As aviary birds, the popular advantage of these parrots over New World birds is that their calls are less harsh. The following species are commonly kept:

Brown-headed parrot *(P. cryptoxanthus)* • These birds have brown plumage that extends over the head, silvery-grey ear coverts, and green body plumage, with yellow underwing coverts that are revealed only in flight. During the breeding period, offer softbill food to these birds for rearing their chicks.

Red-bellied parrot *(P. rufiventris)* • Among the most colourful of the poicephalid parrots, the red-bellied parrot is the only one of its species that can be

cock   hen

Forpus parrotlets can be housed in an outdoor aviary all year round.

sexed visually. Cock birds have orange plumage on their lower underparts and contrasting brown body plumage, while hens are bluish-green. Although pairs tend to be nervous, especially when breeding, they are quite prolific once they are settled in their quarters. Any chicks that are hand reared are likely to become very tame.

Jardine's parrot *(P. gulielmi)* • This bird, the largest member of the group, is an attractive shade of green, with black and orange markings in its plumage.

Meyer's parrot *(P. meyeri)* • Meyer's parrot is greyish-brown on the head and wings, with bluish-green underparts and yellow patches at the bend of each wing and over the thighs. Several distinctive subspecies of Meyer's parrot have variations in the colour of their plumage, some with a yellow patch on the crown. However, none of the plumage markings can be used for sexing these birds.

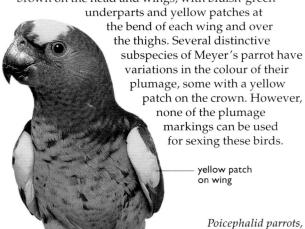

yellow patch on wing

Poicephalid parrots, like this Meyer's parrot, are popular aviary birds. Although they are generally quieter than many parrots, they may resort to attacking woodwork in the aviary.

Senegal parrot (*Poicephalus senegalus*) • The call of this bird consists of a series of attractive whistling notes. Its distinctive orangish-yellow underparts vary in depth of colour according to the individual and cannot be used for sexing. Young birds, recognizable by their dark irises, often develop into excellent companions. Senegal parrots have powerful bills that are capable of destroying thin wire, so make sure that their aviary is fitted with 16-G mesh. The timber frame also needs to be well-protected from their bills. Some pairs tend to breed in early winter, so make sure that the nest box is sheltered. It is best to house individual pairs separately and site the nest box in a secluded and relatively dark corner, using a deep grandfather-clock design of nest box (see page 74).

HANGING PARROTS

Hanging or bat parrots (*Loriculus* spp.) are named after the unusual way in which they roost by hanging upside down from a branch. This behaviour conceals them from birds of prey in their native habitat, but exposes them to attack by foxes and cats in aviaries when they hang onto the mesh. Two popular species are:

Blue-crowned hanging parrot (*L. galgulus*) • This is probably one of the most widely kept members of the group and can be sexed by sight.

Vernal hanging parrot (*L. vernalis*) • Another popular species of hanging parrot, the vernal is noted for its green plumage. These birds can be sexed by the colour of the irises which are distinctly brownish in the hen and whitish in cock birds.

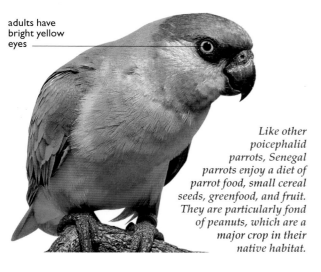

adults have bright yellow eyes

Like other poicephalid parrots, Senegal parrots enjoy a diet of parrot food, small cereal seeds, greenfood, and fruit. They are particularly fond of peanuts, which are a major crop in their native habitat.

blue crown

red throat absent in hen

red rump

cock

The blue-crowned hanging parrot has a brush-tipped tongue for gathering nectar, but will also eat flowers, fruit, and seeds, sometimes while hanging upside down.

It is possible to keep and breed hanging parrots alongside non-aggressive softbills of a similar size, such as zosterops (see page 35). Like softbills, they have a liquid diet based on nectar, with a high fruit intake, which means that their quarters soon become messy and need to be cleaned frequently. A flight cage with solid sides prevents the droppings being sprayed through the mesh, and metal cages coated with epoxy resin are particularly suitable as they can be cleaned easily without the risk of rusting. Remember to trim any overgrown claws (see pages 109), to prevent birds from becoming ensnared in the mesh-panelled roof of a flight.

Hanging parrots enjoy bathing to such an extent that they have been known to take a dip in their nectar if it is served in an open container. To avoid this problem, do not use open containers for liquid food and provide a pot of clean water daily for bathing. It is also important to fix the bath and food well off the ground, as hanging parrots instinctively dislike coming down to the floor of their quarters.

In temperate areas, it is best to bring these birds into a heated bird room or similar over the winter. It is also worth noting, that hanging parrots tend to breathe very fast, but this is not a sign of stress.

Breeding hanging parrots

Hanging parrots thrive in planted flights and, unlike most other parrots, cause no harm to the vegetation. Provide a budgerigar-type nest box in spring when the birds are ready to breed. During the breeding season, they like to use cut leaves to line their nest box, carrying them among the plumage of their flanks. Provide hens with branches of fresh green leaves for this purpose, and build up a thick lining of up to 3.75cm (1.5in) deep in the bottom of the nest. Hens lay on a daily basis, rather than on alternate days.

Parakeets

Parakeets tend to be more widely kept as aviary birds rather than as household companions. This is especially true of Australian species, which are rather nervous creatures and do not settle well within the confines of a cage.

GRASS PARAKEETS

 5–6 🥣 19 🐦 35

The quiet nature of grass parakeets (*Neophema* spp.) makes them highly sought after for aviaries in urban areas as they are unlikely to disturb neighbours. Their attractive coloration, boosted by an ever-increasing range of colour mutations and their readiness to breed, has also helped to establish their popularity.

Splendid grass parakeet (*N. splendida*) • These birds are also known as scarlet-chested grass parakeets because of the cock bird's brilliant-red chest plumage. This coloration is salmon-pink in dilute forms.

Turquoisine grass parakeet (*N. pulchella*) • This stunning parakeet breeds readily, but pairs tend to be quite aggressive and are best housed on their own.

Bourke's grass parakeet (*N. bourkii*) • The brown, pink, and violet-blue in this parakeet's plumage is unusual among parrots. The rosa mutation shows an even greater amount of pink feathering than the normal.

Blue-winged grass parakeet (*N. chrysostomus*)
Elegant grass parakeet (*N. elegans*) • These two less-colourful species have olive-yellow underparts and wings, marked with blue along the outer edge of the wing and in a bar across the forehead.

hen

cock

The vivid colours of these splendid grass parakeets have greatly increased their popularity in aviaries and stock is widely available.

The golden-mantled rosella, sometimes abbreviated to GMR, is now bred in a variety of colour forms, including a rare lutino form, with a yellow-and-white body and red head.

ROSELLAS

5–7 🥣 21 🐦 35

Rosellas (*Platycercus* spp.) have distinctive scalloped patterning on the wing feathers. Two popular species are the golden-mantled rosella (*P. elegans eximus*) and the crimson rosella or Pennant's parakeet (*P. elegans*), which is brick-red with blue on the cheeks and outer edges of the wings. The smallest member of the group is the western rosella or Stanley's parakeet (*P. icterotis*), which measures about 25cm (10in) from beak to tail.

Rosellas need long flights, of 1.8m (12ft) or more in length, and pairs should be housed on their own as they can be aggressive. Hen western rosellas are easily identified by their green, rather than orangish head and underparts, but visual sexing can be more difficult in other species. Pairs usually nest readily when they reach maturity at about twelve months.

OTHER AUSTRALIAN PARAKEETS

The Princess of Wales' parakeet (*Polyteius alexandrae*), with its striking pastel shades, and the red-rumped parakeet (*Psephotus haematonotus*), both need similar care to the rosellas. Though quite hardy, they may develop respiratory problems during prolonged damp weather. These parakeets are also prone to intestinal roundworms, acquired when foraging on the ground.

hen

cock

Plum-headed parakeets are ideal for garden aviaries, even in an urban area.

PSITTACULID PARAKEETS

🐦 ⬜ 🥚 3–6 🥣 25–9 🐤 49–60

Psittaculids tend to roost outside in the breeding period, making them vulnerable to frostbite. There are 14 species, of which some of the most popular are:

Ring-necked parakeet (*Psittacula krameri*) • The native habitat of this bird ranges from north Africa through to China. The African form (*P. k. krameri*) differs from the Indian (*P. k. manillensis*) by its dark upper bill.

Alexandrine parakeet (*P. eupatria*) • Although quite noisy and destructive, Alexandrines look spectacular in aviaries. They prefer deep nest boxes with a layer of wood chips that they can use to line the nest.

Plum-headed parakeet (*P. cyanocephala*) • This species is less destructive than other psittaculids and has an almost musical call. It is gentle enough to be housed with finches in a large flight, and is ideal for garden aviaries. Pairs nest in warm weather, but chicks are prone to chilling because hens stop brooding at night before their offspring are fully feathered. These birds produce only one round of eggs per breeding season, even if the clutch fails to hatch.

Slaty-headed parakeet (*P. himalayana*) • These grey-headed birds can be visually sexed by means of the maroon wing patches on cock birds. Young birds can be identified by their green head plumage.

Moustached parakeet (*P. alexandri*) • This bird has a mostly green body with salmon feathering on the breast and dark markings along its lower bill. Hens have black bills, but this feature varies in subspecies.

BROTOGERIS PARAKEETS

🌐 🐦 ⬜ 🥚 4–5 🥣 27 🐤 45–50

These squat, fruit- and seed-eating birds include the canary-winged parakeet (*Brotogeris versicolurus chiriri*) and the tovi or bee-bee parakeet (*B. jugularis*). Provide a range of perches in the aviary to prevent birds gnawing the framework, and house breeding pairs individually.

BOLBORHYNCHUS PARAKEETS

🐦 ⬜ 🥚 3–7 🥣 18 🐤 35

Slimmer and quieter than brotogeris parakeets, the barring on the lineolated species (*Bolborhynchus lineola*) cannot be used for sexing.

CONURES

🌐 🐦 ⬜ 🥚 3–8 🥣 26 🐤 56

Interest in conures, which originate in Central and South America, has increased dramatically in recent years. Their only drawback is that they tend to be noisy. The three main types of conure available are:

Patagonian conure (*Cyanoliseus patagonus*) • This loud bird resembles a macaw, but lacks the bare cheek patches. The body is olive green with a dark grey chest scattered with white, and golden underparts.

Aratinga conures • Many aratingas have red head plumage, while the golden-crowned or peach-fronted aratinga (*A. aurea*) has different coloured head markings and green body plumage. Visual sexing is impossible as the colours do not reflect gender. Pairs nest readily and hand-reared chicks make good pets for children.

Coloration varies between individual birds

Pyrrhura or scaly-breasted conures • The chest markings of these birds stand out from the green body plumage. Being quiet, they are well suited to garden aviaries, and often become tame. Nesting pairs are likely to be prolific and are quite hardy.

*The sun conure (*A. solstitialis*) is the most spectacular of the aratinga conures.*

Large parrots

Time, money, and space are essential resources for keeping large parrots, whether you are seeking a pet or a breeding pair. If such an undertaking does not deter you, however, then you will find that these birds will become lifelong companions.

MACAWS

⊘ ▢ ▢ ♧ 2–3 🥣 25–8 🐦 63–90

Green-winged (*Ara chloroptera*) and blue-and-gold macaws (*A. ararauna*) are some of the largest members of the parrot family, and have notoriously powerful beaks and loud calls. If you are considering keeping macaws, although multi-coloured macaws are the most spectacular in this group, you might find dwarf species such as the yellow-collared macaw (*A. auricollis*) or Hahn's macaw (*A. n. nobilis*), sometimes known as a 'mini macaw', more practical.

If you assume a parental role with young hand-reared macaws, they can develop into superb companions and may even learn to mimic a few words; however, without constant supervision, they are likely to become mischievous vandals.

Macaws kept as aviary birds need to be housed in robust and secure enclosures, as their loud calls often attract bird thieves. The birds tend to destroy branches quickly, so set perches in the floor of the flight as these are easier to replace with vertical uprights and can fully support the bird's weight. Do not worry if your macaws prefer to climb around their quarters rather than fly, as this is normal behaviour for these birds.

AMAZON PARROTS

⊘ ▢ ▢ ♧ 3–4 🥣 25 🐦 49

The Amazon parrots (*Amazona* spp.) originally come from South America and some parts of the Caribbean. It takes several years for them to achieve adult coloration and a young, double yellow-headed Amazon (*A. ochrocephala*) will have a green rather than a yellow head. Among the popular Amazons are the orange-winged (*A. amazonica*) which has orange markings on its flight and tail, and a horn-coloured bill, and the larger blue-fronted (*A. aestiva*) with red-marked

The green colouring on the wings of the green-winged macaw distinguishes these macaws from the Scarlet macaw (A. macao), which has a noticeable area of yellow on the wings. Although their calls are loud and raucous, unlike some macaws, green-winged macaws do not usually screech for prolonged periods during the day.

flight and tail feathers and a black bill. They may live for up to a century. The smallest member of this group is the white-fronted or spectacled Amazon (*A. albifrons*), which has red feathering around its eyes. Unlike other Amazons, this species can be sexed visually, as cock birds display red wing edging, while hens show green.

Head markings are highly variable in this group of birds, especially within the yellow-fronted species (*A. ochrocephala*) and subspecies whose adults have bright yellow areas at the back of their heads which are otherwise green.

The plain-coloured mealy Amazon together with the blue-crowned species (*A. f. guatemalae*) from Central America rank among the noisiest members of the entire group.

When choosing an Amazon as a pet, look for a young hand-reared bird. Try to obtain a young hen if possible because adult cock birds tend to become rather assertive in the breeding period and may bite. Amazon parrots are noisy birds, given to regular periods of screeching at dawn and dusk which may test the tolerance of you and your neighbours. Position the nest box in an aviary so that you can feed the parrots without venturing close, otherwise cock birds may become aggressive and attack you when you approach. If you need to inspect the interior of the nest box, try to distract the birds elsewhere, or arrange a setup with a sliding hatch that allows you to look inside without having to enter the aviary.

PIONUS PARROTS

Pionus parrots are slightly smaller and quieter than Amazons, and are quite talented mimics. They include the attractive blue-headed parrot (*Pionus menstruus*), which has a violet-blue plumage on its head. The remainder of its body colour is predominantly green, with the exception of red feathering under the tail. Adult pionus parrots are often shy but young birds that are raised by hand develop into excellent companions.

AFRICAN GREY

Although the African grey parrot (*Psittacus erithacus*) is widely acknowledged as a superb mimic, it has a tendency to be shy and does not always perform well in front of strangers. The smaller, darker form of the red-tailed grey, known as the Timneh grey (*P. e. timneh*), is less popular among bird-keepers.

Once acclimatized, these and the majority of parrots are hardy, but this process takes time. Pairs of grey parrots can be kept outside all year round, but they need to retreat to a snug, well-lit shelter in bad weather. You may notice that your birds appear uncomfortable during prolonged spells of cold, damp weather.

The bright orange feathering on the wings of the orange-winged Amazon parrot is most noticeable when the wings are held open, often as a display of aggression.

tail flaring

The umbrella cockatoo is so called because of its spectacular umbrella-like crest, which it can raise and fan out at will.

African grey parrots may breed at any stage through the year, especially if housed indoors in a suitable breeding setup. Compatibility is an essential factor when breeding these birds. Should a pair fail to nest, you could consider reallocating the pairs after two years, so that they have new partners. In some cases, this can result in very rapid breeding, with hens producing fertile eggs within several weeks.

COCKATOOS

Cockatoos are spectacular birds and are well suited to aviaries, but they are noisy. Pairs must also be compatible for breeding to be successful, because otherwise the hen may even be killed by her intended partner rather than simply ignored. If you want to breed these parrots, it is worth seeking out a proven pair, rather than purchasing odd individuals in the hope that they bond together. Breeding problems are probably less likely to arise in the case of the umbrella cockatoo (*Cacatua alba*) compared with the attractive pink-feathered Moluccan (*C. moluccensis*) or the lesser sulphur-crested cockatoo (*C. sulphurea*).

Take care when inspecting the cockatoos' nest box in the breeding season, as cock birds often resent this intrusion and may not hesitate to bite you. Only two eggs are laid, and once the chicks hatch, it is common for only one of them to survive through to fledging. The strongest chick usually takes the greater share of the food, leaving its nest mate to become progressively weaker. To ensure that both chicks survive, it is a good idea to remove the smaller one and rear it by hand.

Preparing for a new bird

Before bringing a new bird into your home, you need to find out what kind of housing and diet your bird prefers and equip yourself with the basic essentials for bird-keeping. Once you have prepared for your new arrival, you will have a firm foundation on which to build a successful relationship with your pet.

Choosing a suitable cage for pet birds

The choice of cages on the market today has never been greater, partly because of increased demand from pet-owners with hand-reared parrots. Always choose the largest possible cage so that your bird has adequate space for exercise within its quarters, even if you intend to let it out into a room on a regular basis. Birds with long tails, such as macaws, will require a tall cage. Ultimately, if a bird is confined to a cage that is too small for comfort, it is likely to to start plucking its feathers. The bird will also be at greater risk of obesity through lack of opportunity to exercise, and this could shorten its life expectancy.

FLIGHT CAGES

Cages that enable birds to fly between perches, known as flight cages, are ideal, particularly if they can be enlarged with extra panels. When choosing a cage, note the spacing of the bars. In some large cages, the distance between bars is increased in proportion to the size of the cage. This can be dangerous for small birds, which could get their head stuck between the bars.

If the design of your cage makes a stand necessary, choose one that cannot be toppled easily, especially if you have young children who might try to reach the bird and pull the cage over. Large cages are cumbersome, so look for a stand with castors for better manoeuvrability. Base stands tend to be more stable than those that support the cage from overhead.

Design features

Parrots of all types, including budgerigars, often spend part of their day climbing around their quarters. For this reason, it is better to choose a cage fitted with horizontal rather than vertical bars, as your bird will find it easier to climb and grip the cage sides.

Ease of cleanliness is a very important feature. Your cage should be fitted with a sliding floor tray to make it possible to change the floor covering without difficulty. Ensure that there is a gap between the cage sides and the base of the tray that allows pieces of spilt food, such as chunks of apple, to be removed easily. Otherwise the debris is left behind on the cage floor whenever the tray is removed for cleaning. Where a metal tray is provided with the cage, check that none of the sides are bent, as these create gaps where a bird's feet might become trapped. The edges of thin sheet metal are very sharp, so make sure that they are not exposed and likely to cause injury to a bird's toes.

MAKING THE CAGE SECURE

Unfortunately, the fact that a cage is expensive does not necessarily guarantee that it will be free of problems. The design of cage doors can often be a major point of weakness. Many parrots in particular soon learn how to undo a simple closing device by watching their owners. When the bird becomes bored and is left on its

---

BUYING A CAGE CHECKLIST

When buying a new cage there are so many things to consider. Here are some useful points to look for:
- **size** – is the cage large enough for your birds?
- **bars** – horizontal bars are best for birds. If they are too widely spaced, they could be dangerous.
- **sliding tray** – enables floor covering to be changed easily. If this is metal, check there are no sharp edges.
- **secure door** – must fit well with a secure fastener.
- **wheels or a stand** – wheels make a large cage easy to move, while stands should be strong and stable.

own, it is likely to attempt to imitate the operation and open the door. If your pet is successful, you may come home to find that your furniture has been gnawed and that precious ornaments have been knocked over and broken. Your bird could also injure or poison itself, by flying into a window or nibbling at a deadly houseplant in the room.

Some cages that have a nut fitted on the outside to keep the door closed may appear to be a safe option. Be warned, however, that an intelligent parrot such as the African grey may successfully use a combination of its bill and tongue to loosen the nut from inside the cage, especially if the nut has not been secured tightly.

Blocking escape routes

Budgerigar cages often have spring-closing doors but, although these work well initially, the spring usually weakens after a period of use. The resultant gap that emerges between the edge of the door and the cage front offers sufficient space for the bird to slip through and escape. Special reinforcement clips for spring-closing doors are available from well-stocked cage

retailers, and should help to keep the cage secure. One recommended alternative for parrot owners is to invest in a small combination lock that you can fit around the door and attach to the side of the cage.

Another potential escape route in a bird cage is the opening provided for food and water containers. Most cages are supplied with at least two open plastic pots, which are attached to the sides or ends of the unit. These can be lifted out and refilled from outside the cage. Yet again, the intelligence of parrots proves to be a drawback because the birds often learn how to lift up the grid at the back of the feeding area, causing the pots to fall out of the cage. This is likely to leave the bird without food or water, and provide an opening through which it may be able to wriggle free. To prevent this, make sure that the pots are fixed in place more securely, by using a twisted strand of wire. This keeps the sliding opening closed at all times, except when you are attending to the bird's needs. Budgerigar cages with plastic bases tend to be more secure, because they have flaps that drop down over the opening when the pot is removed.

SITING A CAGE IN A ROOM

Once you have selected a suitable cage and got it home, unpack the unit carefully and wash it off with warm water to ensure that it is thoroughly clean. You can then start to assemble it.

When deciding where to site your cage, look for a relatively quiet area, where the bird can feel secure in its quarters.
• Hang a plastic-covered backcloth on nearby walls to protect them from droppings and water splashes. This fabric is commonly used for plastic tablecloths and a wide range of designs is available.
• Do not site the cage in a kitchen, where toxic fumes may prove fatal.
• Keep the cage out of direct sunlight and draughts.
• Place the cage just below eye-level where you can talk to the bird and let it feed from your hand.
• Support the cage on a secure stand or on a piece of furniture.
• Make sure that cats and other pets cannot reach the cage.

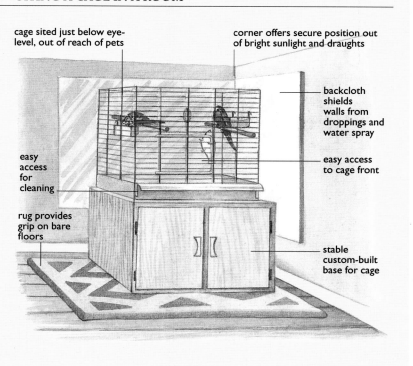

cage sited just below eye-level, out of reach of pets

corner offers secure position out of bright sunlight and draughts

backcloth shields walls from droppings and water spray

easy access for cleaning

rug provides grip on bare floors

easy access to cage front

stable custom-built base for cage

An outdoor aviary and bird room

In temperate climates, spring is the best time to erect an aviary. If you find the thought of constructing an aviary rather daunting, opt for a ready-prepared model in sectional form for which you simply need to lay foundations and join the sections together. Some prolific birds, such as cockatiels, peach-faced lovebirds, and zebra finches, are likely to breed within the first 12 months in a new aviary, but large parrots may take several years to settle in new quarters before nesting.

When looking to buy a sectional aviary, study several manufacturers' catalogues to see the choice of designs available and the price range. Straight comparisons between models can be misleading and you should check timber dimensions. Flimsy frameworks will obviously be cheaper, but less durable. When you are ready to make your choice, it is a good idea to visit the manufacturer to check the quality of the products.

TIMBER-FRAMED FLIGHTS

When considering a timber-framed aviary, check whether the panels are jointed, or simply screwed or nailed together. Jointing is the best option, especially where relatively thin timber is used to form the panels as it helps to prevent the wood from twisting and pulling apart. Make sure that the timber has been made weather-proof with a suitable, safe preservative, which is essential to prolong the lifespan of the aviary.

PLANNING YOUR AVIARY

The size and model of aviary you choose depends on the type and number of birds you intend to keep, your budget, and location.

Most aviaries comprise two parts: the flight, a mesh-covered area open to the elements where birds can exercise; and the bird shelter, where birds are fed and encouraged to roost. This area needs to be well-lit. If you intend to exhibit birds, you are likely to need a bird room for storing food and equipment. A safety porch that leads outside from the aviary stops birds escaping as you enter.

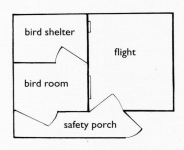

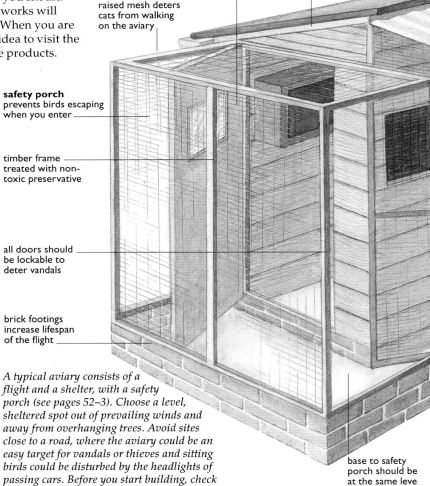

raised mesh deters cats from walking on the aviary

bird room door opens outwards for easy access

bird room for breeding cages and/or storage

safety porch prevents birds escaping when you enter

timber frame treated with non-toxic preservative

all doors should be lockable to deter vandals

brick footings increase lifespan of the flight

base to safety porch should be at the same leve as the aviary

A typical aviary consists of a flight and a shelter, with a safety porch (see pages 52–3). Choose a level, sheltered spot out of prevailing winds and away from overhanging trees. Avoid sites close to a road, where the aviary could be an easy target for vandals or thieves and sitting birds could be disturbed by the headlights of passing cars. Before you start building, check that you do not need planning permission.

If you are considering the less-expensive option of an aviary made from untreated timber, you need to take into account the time and additional cost of applying the preservative yourself and allowing the wood to dry thoroughly before it can house birds. Moreover, treating the timber can be quite difficult once the mesh is in place on the framework.

bird shelter
where birds can roost and be fed

flight where birds can exercise

natural-wood perches deter birds gnawing flight frame

guttering and sloped roof directs rain water away from the flight

mesh is attached to the flight on the inner surface

floor slopes away from shelter for good drainage

:ty porch door :ns outwards

Mesh

The thickness of the mesh gauge and the dimensions of the strands also have an influence on the cost of aviary panels. Most panels are clad with 2.5 x 1.25cm (1 x 0.5in), 19-gauge (19G) mesh. This strand size is usually sufficient to exclude all mice, while still being able to accommodate small birds such as waxbills. It is also usually strong enough for larger birds such as cockatiels, budgerigars, and grass parakeets. However, if you want to house conures, use 16-gauge (16G) mesh. Most aviary manufacturers are able to make up special-size panels to order.

Thanks to the weather and the weight of birds holding on to the mesh, ordinary panel staples are likely to work loose and, ultimately, provide openings through which birds may escape. For this reason, special curved netting staples, which offer a more secure means of attachment, are preferable. Make sure, too, that the finish on the inner face is covered with battening. This protects birds from any loose ends of mesh, which can cause injury especially if they catch on leg rings. If the mesh has not been cut back tightly, apply battening around each frame with special panel pins, which do not split the wood.

METAL-FRAMED FLIGHTS

The destructive nature of large parrots makes them better suited to metal-framed rather than timber flights. Metal frames need to be bolted together on a secure base, typically made of blockwork or bricks, and often with 14-gauge (14G) mesh covering the panels. Choosing a mesh with wide spacing to offset the increased cost of thicker wire, may prove to be a false economy if it allows mice to over-run the aviary. Keep to mesh that is no larger than 2.5sq cm (1sq in), otherwise, unwelcome visitors, such as rats and wild birds, can gain access to the aviary and may introduce diseases and parasites; rats are also known to attack birds in their nest boxes.

SPECIAL DESIGNS

If you want a particular design of aviary, then sketch out the dimensions carefully on paper. It is advisable to bear in mind that panels are normally built to a standard width of 91cm (3ft), as this corresponds to the roll width of the mesh used, making it the most economical option. For this reason, custom-built panels with a special size will be more expensive.

SHELTERS

Most bird-keepers favour full-length shelters, as these shed-like structures are easy to access. There has, however, been a recent trend to provide raised shelters, supported by pillars of bricks or concrete blocks. Although raised shelters require less timber and are less expensive to build, their main drawback is that you have to enter the aviary through the flight whenever you need to attend to your birds. Unless the flight area is large, this kind of traffic can distress any nervous pairs and prevent them from breeding.

Adequate provision of windows will persuade birds to use the shelter. Position one window at the back so you can check where the birds are before entering, and a smaller window at the side. Screen windows with mesh so you can open them safely for ventilation.

GETTING IN AND OUT OF YOUR AVIARY

The number of entry points to an aviary affects your initial outlay and needs to be considered carefully. In most cases, one external door only is necessary in a small aviary, opening into the back of the shelter. An internal door should lead from the front of the shelter and open out into the flight itself to give you easy access for cleaning or for catching your birds.

Safety porch

A safety porch is a wise investment and serves to traps any birds that slip through the aviary door when you open it to enter. It is not an attractive feature, mostly comprising a wire-mesh framework, so try to conceal it at the back of the structure. Hinge the outer door of the safety porch to open outwards, so that access is less awkward when you are carrying equipment or food.

Locks and bolts

Aviaries are not usually equipped with locking devices, so you need to fit these separately. Where bolts are used, remember to keep them well oiled to deter rust and to ensure that they do not freeze on cold nights.

USING PLANTS

Soften the lines of a safety porch by planting fast-growing climbing shrubs such as Russian vine (*Polygonum baldschuanicum*) around the base of the porch. Trim this back as necessary, to prevent the weight of the plant from damaging the structure. Train climbing annuals such as nasturtiums to grow up a mesh, to define a barrier such as a flight screen.

BOX-TYPE AVIARY

Reminiscent of the designs favoured in the Victorian period, box-type aviaries are suitable for keeping small birds such as finches in relatively exposed areas. They have a full-length shelter, and are fully panelled in wood with the exception of one meshed length of the flight. A shallow bird bath on the floor of the flight allows birds to bathe without being exposed to the worst of the weather. This type of aviary also suits nervous birds, as unwelcome visitors cannot climb on the roof and disturb them.

BENEFITS OF A BIRD ROOM

While a garden shed can obviously be converted into a separate bird room, it helps if the bird room and aviary are combined. This type of setup, in which the aviary shelter is incorporated into the bird room, and entered through the bird room itself, greatly reduces the risk of birds escaping. A well-designed bird room can also provide space for breeding cages, and even an indoor flight for young or sale stock.

Arranging space, heat, and light

When planning your bird room, make sure you provide adequate cupboard space and shelving for the storage of seed, show cages, and other bird-keeping equipment. You might also find a power supply helpful, particularly during the winter months.

A sink provides easy access to water, for both feeding and cleaning, but remember to lag all external pipes to prevent burst pipes in cold winters. It is important that the bird room is easy to clean, especially the floor. Linoleum is ideal for this purpose, and can be stuck down along the edges with special sealant to prevent it from lifting. Make sure that it is sealed tightly to keep out dirt, seed husks, or mites, which can establish themselves in this part of the aviary.

If you decide to heat your bird room, avoid any open flame type of heating, as this is potentially dangerous. Instead, choose an electric convection heater with a thermostat, similar to the tubular models used in greenhouses. Good insulation, such as secondary double glazing and draught excluders, helps to contain heating costs in areas with cold winters. You can also line your bird room with insulation material (used strictly in accordance with manufacturers' recommendations) placed between the outer walls and an inner lining of oil-tempered hardboard, which can be painted.

Lighting in bird rooms is best controlled by a time-switch or photo-electric cell, which operates the lights once daylight falls below a specified level. You might

A typical bird room and aviary

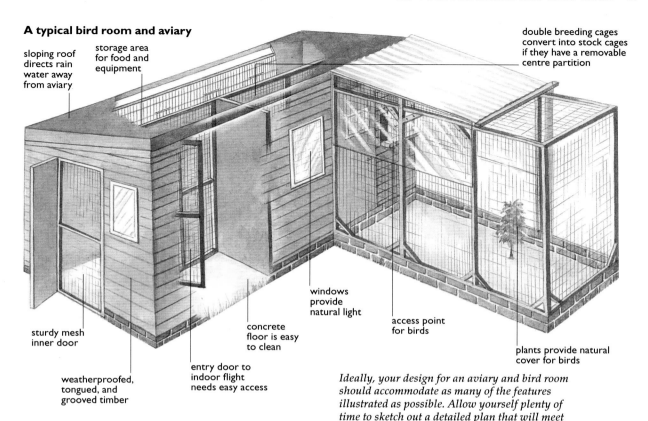

sloping roof directs rain water away from aviary

storage area for food and equipment

double breeding cages convert into stock cages if they have a removable centre partition

sturdy mesh inner door

weatherproofed, tongued, and grooved timber

entry door to indoor flight needs easy access

concrete floor is easy to clean

windows provide natural light

access point for birds

plants provide natural cover for birds

Ideally, your design for an aviary and bird room should accommodate as many of the features illustrated as possible. Allow yourself plenty of time to sketch out a detailed plan that will meet your needs and fully cater for the type of birds that you intend to keep.

DRAWING UP A PLAN

When planning your bird room, space is probably going to be your main consideration. If you have enough room in your garden, try to incorporate the bird room into the design of your aviary. Plan where you are going to position doors and which way they will open. A sturdy, inner mesh door can be used in place of a safety porch and allows the outer door to be left open in warm weather. Mesh-covered windows at the front of the bird room will provide natural light and ventilation. Make sure that you plan enough cupboards and shelving, for storing breeding cages, food, and other equipment.

bird room

shelter

indoor flight

outdoor flight

like to include a dimmer switch in the lighting system too, so that your birds are never plunged suddenly into darkness, which can distress nesting birds that are not at their roost when the lights are turned off in a room.

Roofing

Roofs leak very readily, especially when their protective covering is damaged. When erecting your bird room, take care not to scuff the roofing felt, otherwise water runs back beneath the felt and, before long, a damp stain will appear on the ceiling.

ROUTINE MAINTENANCE

An aviary should last for up to 20 years, provided that it is maintained properly. Oil hinges regularly, replace worn or damaged roofing felt, and treat timber as needed, remembering to remove the birds first. Check guttering for blockages, especially in autumn, because overflows might encourage rot. Such basic checks will prolong the life of your aviary, at little cost or effort.

Building your aviary

Whether you are building an aviary from scratch or assembling a sectioned model, you need to have some DIY knowledge. If you do not feel confident enough to undertake the project, seek the advice of a professional carpenter or experienced bird-keeper.

LAYING THE FOUNDATIONS

Mark out the area carefully with pegs and string. Using a sharp spade, dig out any turf, which can be replanted later if kept moist. Fill the site with compacted hard core and top it with concrete. For secure foundations, set a course of concrete blockwork to a depth of at least 30cm (12in). Above ground level, use bricks for an attractive appearance to the aviary, or face the blocks with mortar and paint them with an exterior paint.

FIXING THE FRAMES

If you intend to anchor the aviary with bolts, set them at intervals of approximately 91cm (3ft) around the base, in wet concrete between the blocks or bricks. Drill

corresponding holes in the bottom of the framework to accommodate these bolts, enabling the washers and nuts to be fixed in place. Try to keep these fixings well-lubricated with oil, in case you need to dismantle the structure at a later date. Frame fixers are easier to use than bolts, as you simply position the pre-drilled frames on the base and knock the frame fixers through into the masonry below. However, bolts are still needed for holding together the frames, which must always be assembled with the mesh on the inner face. This is very important with destructive species, such as budgerigars and other parrots, because the birds are likely to attack the exposed edges of timber and damage the aviary.

Frames tend to be quite heavy and cumbersome, so ask someone to hold them in position while you fix them. Start with adjoining corners, to give greater stability to the structure from the outset, and position the roof section last to bind together the vertical uprights. Although expensive, brass hinges are best for hanging the doors, as they do not rust.

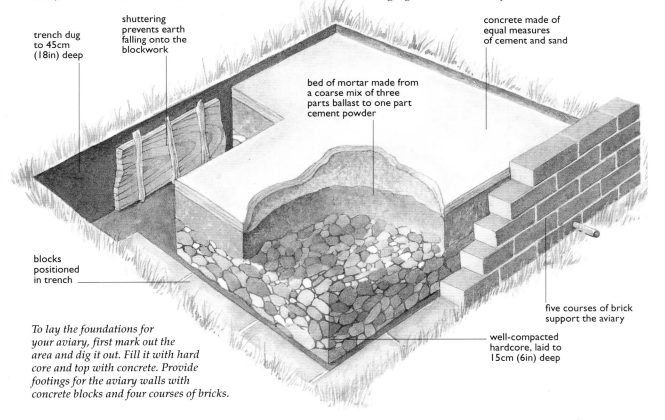

trench dug to 45cm (18in) deep

shuttering prevents earth falling onto the blockwork

concrete made of equal measures of cement and sand

bed of mortar made from a coarse mix of three parts ballast to one part cement powder

blocks positioned in trench

five courses of brick support the aviary

well-compacted hardcore, laid to 15cm (6in) deep

To lay the foundations for your aviary, first mark out the area and dig it out. Fill it with hard core and top with concrete. Provide footings for the aviary walls with concrete blocks and four courses of bricks.

ROOFING

Using special nails, tack heavy-duty roofing felt over timber boarding, or marine plywood for a smoother finish. Overlap the layers so that rain cannot run back and penetrate the woodwork beneath. Seal the joins with waterproofing tape to prevent weather erosion.

Weather protection

Cover the first 91cm (3ft) of flight closest to the shelter with ultra-violet resistant, translucent plastic sheeting at an angle to allow for the run-off of rain water. This material breaks easily, so buy sheeting that is already cut to the desired length, and only use the recommended capped screws to anchor it in place.

Remember that you will need to replace the sheets over time, as they become brittle after prolonged exposure to sunlight. A wooden surface is preferable to plastic in tropical climates and may also suit nervous pairs which are less likely to be disturbed by the sound of cats walking over this area of the roof.

Use additional sheeting on the sides of the aviary to shield against wind, or construct panels covered with plastic sheeting which can be hooked firmly on to the exposed sides of the aviary in cold weather.

DRAINAGE

Fix plastic guttering around the aviary roof at its lowest points to channel rain water into a garden water butt or soak-away. Provide adequate drainage out of the flight so that water does not accumulate, as young fledglings can easily become waterlogged.

FLOORING

Lay a sloping, concrete base, so that rain water quickly runs away through an exit hole at the end opposite the shelter. Alternatively, pave the floor with stone slabs, which can be moved easily if the aviary needs to be relocated at a later date. Both of these surfaces can be cleaned and disinfected without difficulty.

A gravel base is only really suitable for aviaries housing individual pairs of birds, but is difficult to clean of feathers during the moulting period. To collect the accumulation of droppings, place concrete slabs beneath each of the perches. Soil-based coverings are equally difficult to keep clean and infections can spread rapidly. Unless the flight is large, grass is hard to maintain, especially if the drainage is poor, and is likely to be replaced by moss. Use containers for planting up an aviary, so that they can be removed for maintenance. Softbills and finches typically need a planted flight to encourage them to breed.

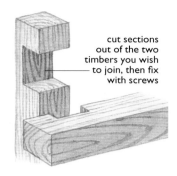

cut sections out of the two timbers you wish to join, then fix with screws

Two timbers can be joined by cutting a cross-halving joint in each with a saw and chisel. Mark the area to be removed on the top and side of the wood. Saw down just inside the vertical lines as far as the depth lines, then chisel out the waste a little at a time. Join the two timbers and fix together firmly with screws.

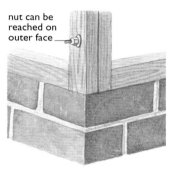

nut can be reached on outer face

Fix the bolts directly and externally through the adjoining faces of timber, fitting both washers and nuts, which need to be oiled regularly to prevent them from seizing up and rusting. With the nuts in this position, they are readily accessible, should you need to dismantle the aviary and reassemble it elsewhere in the future.

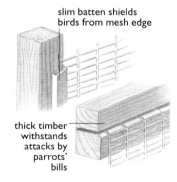

slim batten shields birds from mesh edge

thick timber withstands attacks by parrots' bills

Remove any loose strands of wire, to avoid injury to the birds. The mesh should always be applied to what will form the inner face of the flight, to protect timber from the birds' bills. Use stout battening held in place with panel pins to cover the exposed edges of mesh.

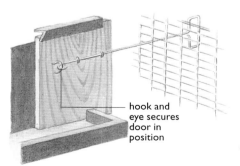

hook and eye secures door in position

A plywood door, set on runners, allows you to keep birds in or out of the shelter. It can be pulled or pushed into position from outside the aviary.

Finishing touches

A wide range of equipment is now available for pet and aviary birds, but it can be expensive and you should be sure you really need it. There are some circumstances where a natural option can be better, particularly in the case of perches.

DRINKERS AND FEEDERS

Although cages are usually equipped with two open pots, it is best to buy a drinker unit so that the second container can be used as a receptacle for non-perishable food. Moreover, these pots are often too flimsy to withstand attack from destructive bills. For small birds, choose a clip-on model that can be attached to the side of the cage. Plastic units of this type are less likely to be contaminated by seed husks or bird droppings, and so ensure a clean supply of water.

Large parrots often try to play with their water containers and dislodge or puncture them. For these birds, use clip-on bottles that are fitted with special metal shields on their fronts to prevent the bird from attacking the bottle and stainless-steel tube that dispenses the water. Stout feeding containers are

A wide range of equipment is available from good pet stores and specialist stalls at bird shows. Prices can vary considerably, so it is always best to shop around.

hygrometer for monitoring the relative humidity of a bird room

cuttlefish is a valuable source of calcium

natural wood perches for birds to gnaw

equally useful for aviary birds, although seed hoppers are more suitable for budgerigars. These feeders can serve several birds at the same time and are fitted with a tray underneath to catch the seed husks before they scatter over the aviary floor.

Offer perishable foods in heavyweight ceramic containers, as they are easy to wash out after use and most birds are unable to tip them over.

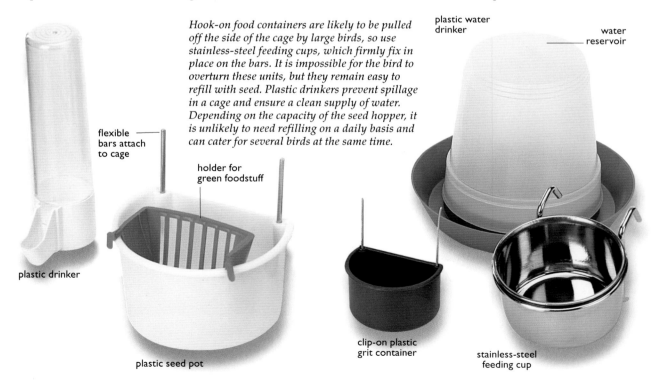

Hook-on food containers are likely to be pulled off the side of the cage by large birds, so use stainless-steel feeding cups, which firmly fix in place on the bars. It is impossible for the bird to overturn these units, but they remain easy to refill with seed. Plastic drinkers prevent spillage in a cage and ensure a clean supply of water. Depending on the capacity of the seed hopper, it is unlikely to need refilling on a daily basis and can cater for several birds at the same time.

flexible bars attach to cage

holder for green foodstuff

plastic water drinker

water reservoir

plastic drinker

plastic seed pot

clip-on plastic grit container

stainless-steel feeding cup

CAGE PERCHES

While plastic perches may appear more hygienic than wooden ones, they do not give parrots the opportunity to exercise their bills and keep them in shape. Birds also seem to find plastic perches uncomfortable for long periods, and cling on to the cage sides for longer than would be expected. The constant diameter of plastic perches is likely to cause a build-up of pressure points on the feet, and these can become sore and infected.

Natural perches, therefore, are a better choice. Select branches from trees such as sycamore, elder, or apple, and avoid those that are poisonous to birds, notably yew and laburnum, as well as any that may have been sprayed recently with chemicals. Make sure that the perches are not too narrow for the bird's grip as they may cause its claws to curl back between the hind toes, and risk the rear of the foot being punctured. Wash the branches before use in case they have been soiled by wild birds, and replace the perches regularly, when they become damaged or soiled.

AVIARY PERCHES

Natural perches suit aviaries too, and should run across the flight, enabling the birds to fly up and down easily. Try to avoid bending the perches against the mesh if possible, as holes are likely to develop. Wire the perches firmly around the vertical supports of the flight, making sure that they are not in a position where a bird is likely to rub its tail against the mesh.

Provide higher perches in shelters, as roosting birds prefer these for security if they are not using a nest box. Where birds are housed in groups, install staged perching in the shelter to offer enough space for most of them to perch. Ready-made units are available, or you can construct them quite easily from dowel. Revolving and other moving perches are generally disliked by birds, although budgerigars may use them. A perch fixed to the top of the cage is a good idea when your bird is out of its quarters, because this is where the bird is likely to rest in between flying around the room.

WARNING

Many birds will spend hours playing with toys, but do not be tempted to leave them unattended. In particular, young budgerigars up to the age of about six months should not be allowed to use toy ladders as they can easily become caught between the rungs.

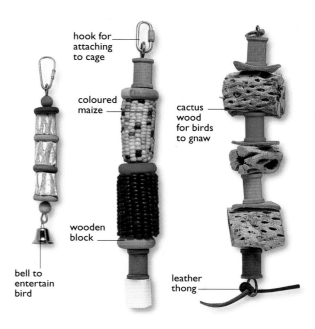

hook for attaching to cage

coloured maize

cactus wood for birds to gnaw

wooden block

bell to entertain bird

leather thong

An increasing variety of colourful toys and chews are available for pet birds. These are usually mainly made from natural materials, such as wood and leather, that the bird can gnaw at to keep its bill in trim. When buying chews, make sure that there are no dangerously small parts.

TOYS

Match your choice of toys closely to the needs of an individual bird as it develops its own preferences, and make sure that the toys are sufficiently robust to withstand attack. Plastic toys designed for budgerigars can prove to be very dangerous for large parrots, which are able to crack and splinter the plastic, sometimes exposing sharp pieces of metal inside. Many parrots like to exercise their bills on knotted leather thongs, unknotting the strands and gnawing the leather. Take care when choosing rope toys, though, because a bird is more likely to swallow any fine strands and these could block its intestinal tract.

Mirrors are popular toys with many birds, but they are not recommended for cock budgerigars during the breeding season. These birds tend repeatedly to feed their reflections, and this can lead to loss of condition. Exercise centres for birds of all sizes typically include climbing frames, wheels, and branches. Most are free-standing and fitted with a base to collect droppings. Choose simple toys such as ping-pong balls, which are more suitable than ornate open-weave balls. Above all, make sure that your pet's toys can be cleaned easily.

Making your home safe

Sadly, pet birds face many potential dangers that are lurking in the home. Worse still, some of these might not always be apparent until it is too late – even the most obvious hazards can sometimes be overlooked.

Keep a close eye on the whereabouts of small birds at all times when they are out of their cages, especially when they are resting. If a bird is very tame and used to sitting on your shoulder or arm, it will not fly away when you approach and you might accidentally sit on the bird if it lands on a cushion. Place perches around your room so that a bird is easy to spot. If you have two parrots housed separately in the same room, it is not a good idea to let just one bird out of its quarters. The confined parrot may become jealous and bite the foot of the other bird if it perches on its cage.

SECURING THE ROOM

Always check thoroughly for escape routes before releasing a bird into a room.

- Make sure that all the windows are closed and screen them with net curtains, if possible, as birds often attempt to fly straight through glass.
- Exclude any pets that could harm your bird when it is free in the room.

- Keep the door to the room closed at all times, and place a notice on the outside of the door to alert other members of the household before they enter.

Household hazards

- Clear the room of all pot plants, including cacti, which could cause physical injury. Many popular houseplants, including ivies and poinsettias, are likely to prove poisonous if ingested by birds. Parrots in particular are often tempted to nibble plants, such as the toxic orange fruits of the winter cherry plant (*Solanum capsicastrum*).
- Remove vases of cut flowers, as these could easily be knocked over by the bird.
- Shield any fires, to prevent any risk of a bird burning itself. This may seem obvious, but a bird's tail feathers can easily pass through the mesh of a fireguard and be singed by flames.
- Cover a disused fireplace with a fireguard. Although a bird is unlikely to escape via a chimney, it is best to seal this off as retrieval would be difficult and messy.
- Cover any aquaria, as these can be dangerous if left uncovered. Your bird could fall in and drown, or it might pick up an infection if it drinks the water.

The kitchen is probably the most dangerous area of the house and, if only on grounds of hygiene, birds should be excluded at all times. There are likely to be hot surfaces and naked flames that will burn the skin, as well as sharp implements and electrical equipment such as dishwashers and microwaves, in which smaller pet birds may accidentally stray and meet an untimely end.
The cooking utensils may also be harmful. Non-stick cookware which, if allowed to overheat, gives off deadly fumes that can prove fatal to birds. Irons and ironing boards are also a source of toxic polytetrafluoroethylene gas, which accumulates in the bird's lungs and can kill.

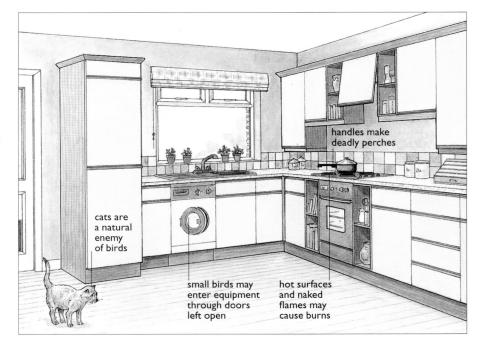

handles make deadly perches

cats are a natural enemy of birds

small birds may enter equipment through doors left open

hot surfaces and naked flames may cause burns

Electrical fittings

Electrical wires present an irresistible target for birds, and large parrots such as Amazons can easily penetrate the coating around the electric wire, with dire results.

If your bird picks up a live electrical wire, never try to persuade the bird to release it, as it is almost inevitable that the bird will respond by tightening its grip. Instead, switch off and disconnect the power supply immediately, and then try to persuade the bird to put down the wire. Once the danger is passed, check that there is no damage to the wire before reconnecting.

• Place all wires out of reach, tucking them down behind other objects.
• Disconnect plugs that are not going to be used while the bird is free in the room.

Dangerous chemicals

Many modern chemicals, from flea sprays to household cleaners, can be fatal to birds, so avoid using them near your pet. Move the bird to another room before cleaning, and leave the windows open until the room is fully ventilated. Do not leave parrots close to painted woodwork in old houses as lead-based paints can kill.

Smoking in close proximity to birds can also harm their health; low-grade respiratory infections are common in birds that live with chronic smokers.

Toilets and bathrooms are dangerous places for birds. If a bird tries to bathe in the toilet or basin its plumage may become waterlogged causing it to drown.

bird may knock over breakable items to reach mirror

houseplant may be toxic

bird may try to bathe in toilet bowl

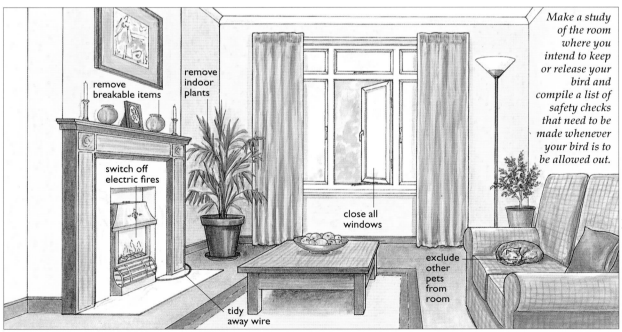

remove breakable items

remove indoor plants

switch off electric fires

close all windows

tidy away wire

exclude other pets from room

Make a study of the room where you intend to keep or release your bird and compile a list of safety checks that need to be made whenever your bird is to be allowed out.

Aviary safety and security

It is important that your birds feel safe in their quarters, especially if you are intending to breed them. To help them settle down in new surroundings, try to follow the same routine each time you enter the aviary. As they learn to recognize your presence you will notice that they become less alarmed and stop flying wildly around their quarters.

For smaller birds, such as finches and softbills, try planting some dense cover in the flight so they can retreat to the foliage if they feel threatened.

Some birds are very nervous by nature and require extra coaxing and patience from their keepers. Pigeons and doves, together with Australian parakeets, often prove to be the most highly strung birds. Their main defence against predators is speed, so they tend to fly off rapidly at the first hint of possible danger.

Birds are most likely to be disturbed at night. If alarmed, a bird might not appreciate the confines of the aviary in the darkness and may end up flying into the mesh at high speed and fatally injuring itself. Young birds that have recently left the nest are particularly vulnerable to this risk.

DEALING WITH UNWELCOME VISITORS

Cats can become a major problem around an aviary. Even without coming into direct contact with the occupants, they can disturb and distress birds by climbing up the panels and walking on the roof. Most garden centres and hardware stores stock deterrents, which you should sprinkle around the aviary to keep cats at bay, renewing the applications after rain.

If your aviary is visited by foxes, check that there are no weaknesses around the aviary floor and that the roof is strong enough to support their weight should they climb up on top of the aviary.

Rodents

Keep a regular check in your aviary for any evidence of rodents, such as mice or rats. Signs can easily be missed, especially if they are simply entering the aviary to feed, rather than taking up residence. Look for droppings near a food pot – these are often mistaken for spilt niger seed – or check any paper lining the flight floor for nibbled edges or yellow patches of urine stain. Rodents are frequently responsible for infections within aviaries, such as yersiniosis (see pages 100–1) and must be eliminated immediately before they establish them-selves and become harder and more costly to eradicate.

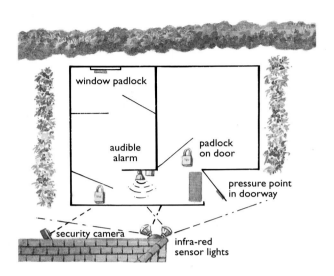

There are now an increasing number of security options available to safeguard aviary premises, and you may be able to seek independent advice from a police crime-prevention specialist. Make sure all entry points are protected, and invest in some practical anti-theft devices.

Traps for mice

You can catch mice either singly in breakback traps, or in live traps, which can take 12 or more mice at a setting. If you decide on breakback traps, to avoid accidentally killing a bird, it is essential to remove all the birds to alternative accommodation, such as a temporary flight in a garden shed. Live traps are popular because they can be used while the birds are still in the aviary. Remove all other sources of food at night to draw the mice into the traps. It may take a week or so to clear them from the aviary, particularly if you are using live traps, which need to be baited for several nights before they can be set.

Once you have three clear nights without catching anything, you can be fairly confident that you have eliminated the pests. Before returning the birds to their quarters hose down the aviary to remove as much dirt as possible, and disinfect thoroughly. Avoid rinsing straightaway because the disinfectant needs a period of contact with the surface in order to be effective as a germ killer. Wash down any perches with a disinfectant, or, better still, replace them, and thoroughly wash food and water pots with the disinfectant solution. Try to trace where the mice entered the aviary and repair the hole. Look carefully around the base of the shelter for any gaps, particularly beneath surrounding vegetation.

Rats

Rats can kill birds directly, particularly at night, and are more likely to burrow into aviaries, so watch for any unusual excavations of soil within or around the perimeter of the aviary. If you suspect the presence of rats in an aviary, it is advisable to remove your birds for their own safety. While you may be successful in catching some rats with traps, you are more likely to need poison for effective elimination. When using a toxic product, place the bait on a tray to minimize the risk of any spillage around the aviary. If you are not confident about using poison, consult a professional pest control firm.

Using ultrasonic scarers

It is possible to deter some animals, such as cats and rodents, from entering the bird room by means of an ultrasonic scarer. This operates at high frequencies, emitting a barrage of sounds that are audible to aviary predators, but cannot be heard by birds or humans. The discomfort of the ultrasonic sounds helps to keep animals out of bird rooms, but there is little prospect of it being effective in the exposed environment of flights.

MAKING THE AVIARY SECURE

Unfortunately, the rise in the prices of birds in recent years has seen a parallel growth in the number of aviary thefts, and there is little prospect of heartbroken owners being reunited with their birds. When you are considering the wide range of security options for safeguarding aviaries, it might be a good idea to seek independent advice from a police crime-prevention officer. This specialist can highlight the essential features of a security system and suggest which types would suit your premises.

Anti-theft devices

Preferably, your security system should be designed to deter thieves before they reach any entry points to the aviary or attempt to cut through the mesh.

Padlock • Although a basic measure, the first step is to fit a secure padlock to the aviary door and possibly windows as a deterrent to casual vandals.

Alarm system • Site hidden pressure pads linked to an alarm system at vulnerable entry points.

Infra-red security lighting • If you decide to install infra-red activated lighting systems along the aviary perimeter, make sure that they are set up properly to prevent false alarms triggered by cats and foxes.

Security cameras • Although a more expensive option, these relay images of the aviary onto a screen in your home, enabling you to check for intruders, especially if you have a silent alarm included in the circuitry.

Dummy cameras • You can enhance an existing alarm system by the addition of dummy cameras which, once mounted in position, are barely distinguishable from a fully functional camera. These decoys are comparatively cheap to buy, yet effective.

DNA profiling • If you are fortunate enough to have your stolen bird recovered, it is vital that you are able to prove its identity. Many bird-keepers use a DNA profiling service offered by laboratories. Also used for the purpose of sexing birds, this test records the DNA profile taken from a sample of the bird's blood.

MICRO-CHIPPING

It is possible to protect individual birds, from about the size of a large finch upwards, by micro-chipping. During this process a tiny micro-chip, which measures about the size of a small grain of rice, is inserted into the muscle of the breast using a special sterile injector. A unique code contained on the chip is logged into a central database, with the owner's details. This code can be read when a special scanner or transponder is placed close to the chip, and enables a lost or stolen bird to be identified easily and returned to its owner.

micro-chip   `7F7E11251E #1`

              scanner reading of identity code

inserting a micro-chip into a bird's breast

Purchasing and caring for birds

Having prepared the accommodation for your new pet, you are ready to purchase the bird of your choice and introduce it to your home. Once the bird has settled into its new surroundings, you can spend time familiarizing yourself with its feeding and behavioural habits, and start to prepare it for exhibitions or breeding.

Where to obtain birds

Once you have decided on the type of bird or birds you wish to keep, you will need to trace suitable suppliers. Most pet stores stock young budgerigars, but few of them are likely to offer the types of budgerigar bred for exhibition. For exhibition birds, such as canaries and society finches, as well as unusual species, you will be better off contacting breeders direct. Regardless of how attractive you might find the idea of owning an exotic or rare species of bird, you should never allow yourself to be tempted to buy wild birds that have been imported illegally. A strict licensing system governed by the Convention on International Trade in Endangered Species (CITES) controls the importation of parrots and other threatened species. If you wish to keep an unusual species of bird, you should seek out a specialist breeder or bird farm.

SOURCING BREEDING SUPPLIERS

The most common starting point for finding a bird stockist is to obtain a selection of current bird-keeping magazines, all of which feature advertisements both from specialist retailers, breeders, and exhibitors who have surplus stock available. You may also find details of the national organization and or regional branches of the body responsible for overseeing the particular breed of bird in which you are interested.

On-site visits

The most satisfactory way of buying is probably to visit the breeders' premises, so that you can see where the birds are being housed and how they are kept. When contacting a breeder, remember to telephone in advance to arrange an appointment, rather than visiting without an invitation. Calling without prior arrangement is likely to be inconvenient for the breeder and, more importantly does not allow for the birds to be caught from a flight in advance, to enable you to see them at close quarters. Unfortunately, the increase of thefts from aviaries has made some breeders wary of visitors, and some do not grant access to their premises. Keep a look out for special club sales and similar events, which are usually advertised in the bird-keeping press, as these are worth attending for the wide choice of stock available.

Knowing what to ask

If you are intending to breed your birds, it is important that you start out with a stock of unrelated individuals, so be prepared to buy from different sources. Do not hesitate to ask the breeder about the birds being offered for sale. You need to know what they are used to eating as a sudden change in diet, together with the stress of being moved to a new environment, could have a serious impact on your bird's health. Try to avoid distress by replicating the diet with which the bird is familiar for at least the first two weeks, before introducing gradual changes. You also need to find out whether the birds have been housed outdoors and are fully hardy, otherwise you may need to provide indoor accommodation for them during the cold winter months in temperate areas.

Selecting your stock

If you are serious about exhibiting birds, you need to be discerning. Inevitably, exhibition stock are more expensive than pet birds, but it is better to start with four or five pairs of the best-quality stock that you can afford, rather than acquiring a greater number of birds of lesser merit. It is always worth considering an individual's pedigree. A bird descended from

Before visiting a breeder write out a list of questions. You should find out as much about a bird as possible before buying.

a top-winning bloodline is likely to pass on the attributes of its lineage, even if it does not measure up exactly to the required standard.

Buying the majority of your foundation stock from one exhibitor means that you can obtain more precise guidance on pairings, but at some stage you will need to obtain unrelated stock. Rather than being dependent on one bloodline, which introduces the risk of problems related to in-breeding, aim to set up with two different family groups. The offspring can be merged gradually and crossed with new additions as your stud expands.

Always be aware of any weaknesses in your stock, and plan pairings accordingly. If your cock bird has an unusually small head but good colour, for example, pair him with a hen that has excellent head quality, even if her coloration is slightly inferior.

LOOKING FOR A PET BIRD

If you want a bird that is going to be easy to tame, such as a parrot or mynah, it is best to choose a genuine young bird. You should try to acquire it after the weaning period when it has become fully independent. Equally, you could select a hand-reared bird, which, although more expensive, has the advantage of already being familiar with a home environment and therefore should settle in readily.

Budgerigars and cockatiels that have not been reared by hand are difficult to tame. However, provided you obtain a young bird, and preferably one that has been handled in the nest, these birds gradually settle down. Young cockatiels tend to be rather wild at first, but soon calm down in domestic surroundings.

Old birds and new tricks

It can be much harder to persuade an older bird that is already able to talk to learn new words from you, so if you want to teach your bird yourself, there is little advantage in acquiring a pet that is already talking well.

Conversely, the bird may have acquired certain words that you do not wish it to repeat. Persuading your pet to lose these from its vocabulary can be difficult, although ignoring the bird and covering its cage for a few minutes immediately after it says the offensive word may act as a deterrent.

What to look for in a bird

Rushing to make a decision about a bird can be costly, so always allow yourself plenty of time to observe and inspect them. In the case of small birds, such as zosterops or tanagers, which cannot be sexed visually, this may enable you to spot a true pair of birds.

COMMON SIGNS

In general, buying young stock is the best way to obtain birds of known age that should breed next year. It can be hard to check young birds, as they tend to sleep more than adults, so look for well-formed droppings on the floor of their quarters as a sign of good health. You can also detect much about a bird's condition from quiet observation. Birds are normally alert and rarely tolerate close approach. If a softbill appears sluggish and slightly fluffed up, it may be off-colour, possibly suffering from a liver ailment or parasitic worms.

clear, bright eye, with no swelling or discharge

nostrils should be unblocked and free from discharge

sleek, well-preened plumage

bill should have no obvious deformities

breastbone should be just discernible, surrounded by muscle on either side

feet should have no signs of swelling or deformity

A healthy bird, like this Chinese hawfinch, should look generally alert, with bright eyes, clear nostrils, and sleek plumage.

Plumage and colour

The condition of plumage is not critical in softbills, as damaged feathers are shed at the next moult. Finches, especially lavender finches *(Estrilda caerulescens)*, are prone to feather-plucking in overcrowded conditions, but the plumage regrows once the birds are removed to more spacious quarters.

Similarly, if a bird's natural coloration appears distorted, as commonly occurs in waxbills, it is not necessarily a cause for alarm. The feathers of the strawberry finch or red avadavat *(Amandava amandava)* often display a black tone which is replaced by red plumage at the next moult.

Feather ailments in parrots may, however, indicate a problem, particularly for cockatoos, which are highly susceptible to psittacine beak and feather disease (see pages 102–3). Any broken or damaged plumage, possibly coupled with an overgrown beak, needs to be treated with suspicion as an infected bird is incurable and presents a hazard to others. Birds showing signs of French moult (see pages 102–3) should also be avoided.

CHECKING THE CONDITION OF YOUR BIRD

Once you have shortlisted your birds, ask for them to be caught up for closer inspection. Holding each bird in a net or your hand, first check its breastbone, which runs down the midline of the body. In a healthy bird it is likely to be just discernible, surrounded on either side by muscle. If there are hollows present on both sides of the breastbone, this is described as 'going light' and warns that the bird is not in good health. Such apparent weight loss is usually a sign that the bird has not been eating properly, or is suffering from parasites or illness.

Eyes and nostrils

Birds are known to disguise eye ailments by watching you out of their good eye, so be sure to examine both eyes closely. Check that there is no discharge and no abnormal swelling present in the surrounding skin.

The nostrils should be unblocked and free from discharge, although hardened food particles may be found in the upper beaks of some softbills. In members of the parrot family, such as grey and Amazon parrots, blocked nostrils suggest an infection in the upper respiratory tract, which can often be linked to a deficiency in vitamin A, arising from a diet of dry seed (see pages 92–3).

Reject any bird with noisy breathing that cannot be linked with an abnormality of the nostrils. It can be hard to distinguish between the wheezing made by pionus parrots when they are restrained and that associated with aspergillosis (see pages 102–3), to which they are susceptible. If you are in doubt, do not buy the bird because there is no truly effective treatment for this chronic illness.

Bill deformities

When checking the bird's bill, make sure that the upper and lower portions meet properly, and that they are not distorted. Overgrown bills tend to be common in some seed-eating pigeons and doves, but they are not a serious problem, compared with undershot beaks in budgerigars, where the upper portion fits inside the lower part of the bill. This deformity may be an inherited weakness so such birds are best avoided, especially if they are intended for breeding purposes.

It is also important, especially with budgerigars and kakarikis (popular parakeets from New Zealand), to check the bill for any early signs of scaly face, which may not have been apparent from some distance away. Treat with suspicion any minute snail-like tracks across the upper bill, as these are early signals of the presence of the mites that cause this infection (see pages 106–7).

Wings and flight

When looking at birds, it is a good idea to open up the wings so that you can inspect the underside of the flight feathers for any congregations of lice close to the central vane. You should also be able to see whether the flight feathers have been clipped. This can be significant, because it handicaps the bird's flying ability until the

dark iris of young parrot

iris becomes paler as parrot matures

One of the common signs to look for when choosing a young parrot is to check its eyes, as the iris colour lightens with age.

next moult. If the wings have been clipped, the bird's accommodation needs to be adjusted so they do not injure themselves when they attempt to fly. They are often best kept in a flight cage rather than an aviary, where they might fall to the floor.

Problems with feet

Check the undersides of the feet of any softbill while the bird is being restrained. If a bird is being kept on a hard perch that has relatively constant diameter, you may see sore areas in the ball of each foot. These pressure pads could become infected, but provided that you are aware of this problem prior to purchase, you can take the necessary steps to ensure a full recovery. Small nectivores, such as sunbirds, need fresh, supple branches for perching to reduce the risk of this problem.

Check the bird's toes carefully, as any permanent injury or missing claws are likely to preclude the bird from being successfully exhibited. This might be an important consideration with some foreign birds. Any overgrown nails can be cut back easily but if swelling of the toes is visible, you need to be more cautious as it might indicate an infection known as bumblefoot. Swelling across one or more joints may signify articular gout, for which successful treatment is likely to be expensive. In the case of gout, treatment is impossible.

VETERINARY CHECKS

You may want to arrange for a veterinary check-up to ensure that all is well with your new bird. There can occasionally be problems relating to the health of hand-raised chicks, such as bone weaknesses resulting from an inadequate rearing diet, although this is uncommon thanks to specially formulated foods.

At the same time, you might like to consider taking out a healthcare policy for your bird, which protects against the costs of veterinary treatment and also offers compensation if your pet is stolen. However, these policies do not cover the cost of routine care, such as nail clipping, and you should always check the exact wording of any document before signing.

Travelling and settling in

When you intend to visit a breeder or a show where stock is for sale, it is always worth taking a wooden box or other bird carrier for transporting any birds that you might buy. The darkened confines of these secure boxes makes the journey less stressful for birds and reduces the risk of their being injured on arrival at their new quarters.

CHOOSING CARRIERS

Special, purpose-built bird carriers, usually of wood, are widely available from pet stores and suppliers. Most models come equipped with perches, ventilation holes, and a wire sliding front that you can remove easily to wash and disinfect the interior when needed. Carriers such as these are very versatile and are as useful for transferring birds between an aviary and bird room as when travelling to exhibitions.

A less-durable alternative to these purpose-built carriers are cardboard containers, which are often supplied flatpacked. These are useful for housing small birds like finches, but should not be used for birds that are likely to gnaw through the cardboard.

Home-made carriers

A plywood box can easily be adapted for use as a secure carrier for parrots and other birds that tend to be destructive, but make sure that ample holes are drilled around the sides to provide ventilation. It is a good idea to fit spacer bars, measuring about 2.5sq cm (1sq in), around the outside of the box to prevent the carrier from being placed too close to walls or other boxes, which would cut off the air supply.

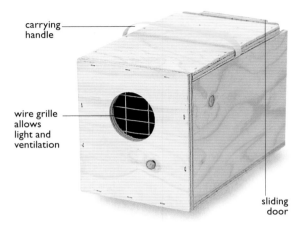

carrying handle

wire grille allows light and ventilation

sliding door

Parrots quickly destroy cardboard with their bills, and so should be carried in a secure wooden box. Ventilation holes should be spaced around the top of the sides out of reach of the parrot's bill, or protected with mesh (shown above).

Large, nervous birds, such as touracos, can be moved successfully in the cardboard boxes that are usually available as packing material in supermarkets. These birds should travel individually, as they might injure each other with their claws. Punch air holes in the box before placing the bird inside, and tape down the roof and flaps with heavy-duty parcel tape. When a bird is first confined in a box, it will often try to take flight and hit the top; however, it is unlikely to harm itself. If the bird gains a foothold on the cardboard, however, it may find an escape route through flaps that are not properly sealed.

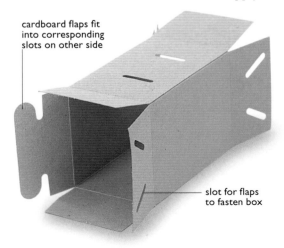

cardboard flaps fit into corresponding slots on other side

slot for flaps to fasten box

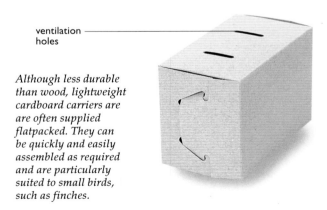

ventilation holes

Although less durable than wood, lightweight cardboard carriers are are often supplied flatpacked. They can be quickly and easily assembled as required and are particularly suited to small birds, such as finches.

TRANSPORTING BIRDS

When travelling by car with your bird, do not be tempted to place it in the trunk. The bird could easily be overcome by deadly exhaust fumes leaking in, or simply become overheated in such stuffy surroundings. Choose a cool part of the car for the bird, preferably on the floor behind the front seats where there is less chance of injury if you have to stop suddenly. Even birds that originate from hot climates have been known to suffer from heat stroke. The temperature inside a parked car can rise to a fatal level within minutes, so never leave your bird in such a deadly furnace during warm weather. If you need to leave your vehicle at any stage, be prepared to take the birds with you.

Provisions for the journey

When placed in the dark confines of a box, birds are less likely to eat or drink, which is not a problem on trips lasting just a couple of hours. Hummingbirds are an exception, in that they need to be able to feed when travelling, otherwise they might be torpid on arrival. For this reason, they are usually carried in cages fitted with nectar drinkers, which should be plastic rather than glass and suspended from the cage roof. You may find that sunbirds need nectar during a journey too, since they also have a high energy requirement. It is best to carry these birds in individual compartments, as they tend to be aggressive when housed together.

INTRODUCING NEW BIRDS

Once your new bird has arrived home, it should be housed in separate quarters, to minimize the risk of it introducing disease to your collection. Although the new bird might appreciate a companion, it is generally not a good idea to place another bird in its quarters as bullying may arise, especially at the food pot.

Settling in

Newcomers are particularly prone to illness, and must be allowed to settle down with minimal stress. They are likely to encounter unfamiliar microbes in the environment, to which your established birds have become immune, so offer a probiotic to stabilize the bacterial population in the gut, making it much harder for harmful microbes to gain access. Dehydration, which weakens resistance to disease, is common in birds that have been travelling, particular those that attend shows. An electrolyte placed in the drinking water can help them to recover from their travels.

Most birds soon settle down in quiet surroundings and quickly start feeding if left alone. Once a newcomer

is ready to join the aviary, restrict it to the shelter for a few days until it is familiar with its surroundings, and then allow the bird to progress into the flight. Keep a close watch on the newcomer during its first week in the aviary, and site food and water within easy reach.

Changes in diet

Take care not to introduce any significant alteration to a bird's diet within the first few weeks of it moving into new quarters, as this increases the risk of digestive disorders. Nectivorous species are most vulnerable to this type of problem and, if enterotoxaemia develops, the outcome is fatal. It is best to offer your bird the nectar food with which it is familiar for at least the first week. Changes can then be made gradually, by offering two separate nectar mixes in the following weeks. This allows time for the beneficial bacteria that line the gut to adjust to the new diet.

Providing bathing facilities

If your new bird is not hardy enough to be housed outside through the winter, you need to provide bathing facilities during its stay indoors . Softbills and lories like to bathe regularly to keep their plumage in good condition and retain their natural waterproofing. This ensures that they do not become saturated by rain showers when they are returned to outdoor quarters in spring. Bathing can also help to reduce the likelihood of feather plucking. Most parrots will not bathe in a bowl of water in the cage and so may need to be sprayed.

SPRAYING BIRDS

Spraying your bird is best carried out just before you want to clean out its quarters. Remember to remove any food pots beforehand. A clean plant sprayer is ideal for use with parrots, as it produces a fine mist. Fill the bottle with tepid water and direct the nozzle above the bird's head so that the water falls like rain. When treating a bird with an aerosol product, be sure to read and follow the manufacturer's instructions carefully before application.

Catching and handling birds

Whether you are inspecting a bird or transferring it to a carrying box, you first need to be able to catch it. People are often nervous of catching and handling birds, but provided that you are careful and use a suitable net there is no real risk of causing injury. Once you have done the job a few times it will become second nature.

CATCHING AN AVIARY BIRD

To ensure a successful catch, plan your strategy in advance of attempting to net a bird in an aviary. If possible, aim to make your catch in the morning or late afternoon rather than during the heat of the day when the bird is more likely to become distressed. Block off the access hole between the shelter and the flight to prevent the birds from flying in and out beyond your reach, and take down any perches so you can move freely around the aviary. If possible, try to confine birds to the shelter.

Using a net

A variety of nets for catching aviary or pet birds are available from suppliers. When choosing a net, select a size that is suitable for the birds you are keeping, and make sure that the rim of the net is well padded. This helps to reduce the risk of injury if a bird collides with the net when you are trying to catch it.

Although it may be possible to catch a bird in flight, it is usually easier to net it while it is holding on to the mesh. As you approach the bird try to find a position that makes it difficult for it to fly past you. Even if you fail to catch the bird at the first attempt, it is likely to fly to the floor, giving you a second chance.

Try to anticipate which direction the bird intends to take, and use your free hand to steer it towards the net. Avoid slamming the net hard against the mesh, as even though it is padded, the rim might injure the bird.

Handling a bird

Once the bird is caught, lower the net to the ground and feel cautiously inside to locate its head. Grasp the sides of the body with your thumb and little finger, enclosing

To catch a bird in an aviary, wait until it has settled on the mesh and then act swiftly.

the wings with the palm of your hand, then place your first and second fingers on either side of the neck so as to restrain the head and stop the bird from biting you. Take care when removing the bird's feet from the net as it is almost certain to tighten its claws and grasp the fabric. Gently pry the claws free and place the bird in a carrying box.

If you find it difficult to make a catch, the bird may start to show signs of distress, such as laboured breathing, pronounced tail movements, and panting with its bill apart. If you become aware of any of these warning signals, allow the bird time to recover before resuming your attempts to catch it.

Checking your bird

If you need to inspect your caught bird, it is best to hold it in your hand so that all parts of the body are readily accessible. A quick check of the bird's overall condition can be carried out by running a finger down the breastbone to detect any hollows. Look at the undersides of the feet and the length of the claws, and make sure that there is no visible staining of the plumage around the vent and on the wings, which should be opened with care, one at a time.

CATCHING A BIRD IN THE HOME

Catching a bird in the home tends to be more difficult than in an aviary because of the obstacles in your way, such as furniture and fittings. A home also offers more vantage points, such as curtain rails and light fittings, where the bird can remain out of your reach.

You may find that you have to catch your bird on a regular basis when you allow it to exercise in a room, as it can be very difficult to persuade a bird to return to its quarters until you have established a routine. Before reaching for a net, you might try to persuade the bird to step on to your hand or outstretched perch and let you carry it back to the cage, although it is very likely to hop off at the last moment and may then climb up on to the top of its cage and fly off again.

Finches and other small birds are quick on the wing and cannot be tamed to the same extent as parrots. This makes them very difficult for one person to catch when they are loose, so try to get someone else to steer the birds while you hold the net ready.

Using your hands

Adopt a more subtle approach than simply chasing your bird around the room. First, draw the curtains together, then place a chair within reach of the curtain rail. Encourage the bird to fly to the rail and, once it has settled, switch off the light, plunging the room into

darkness. Let your eyes get accustomed to the dark, then carefully climb onto the chair and gently reach up to the bird. Cup your hands around its body and when you have it in your grasp, step down from the chair. To ensure a firm hold on a small bird, wrap your fingers around its body.

CATCHING A BIRD IN A CAGE

A cage is probably the easiest environment in which to catch a bird, once it has been cleared of all perches, toys, and free-standing food pots. Use one hand to catch the bird, and remember to keep your free hand around the opening of the door when you reach into the cage. This should prevent any risk of the bird slipping past you if you are unable to catch it at your first attempt.

HANDLING A PARROT

Parrots can be quite a problem to handle, simply because you need to contend with their bills and their powerful wings at the same time – even tame individuals may resort to biting anyone who attempts to catch them. It is better, therefore, to eliminate the need to catch your bird by training it to climb on to your hand at your request. It is worth taking the time to teach your bird this process, as it will allow you to remove and return your bird to its quarters without any stress or harm to either party.

Sometimes a greater degree of restraint is necessary: for example, when the bird needs to undergo close examination by a vet. In these cases, you may find that a towel helps to simplify the handling process. Once you have the bird firmly in your grip, wrap a towel around its body, taking care to fold the wings. Being bound in this way prevents the bird from flapping its wings and keeps its claws out of harm's way. The bird is less likely to struggle once it is restrained, and this allows you to concentrate on avoiding any attack from its bill. If the bird does manage to grasp onto you with its bill and refuses to let go, loosen your grip slightly and it should respond by releasing you from its hold.

Taming, training, and showing your bird

While your bird is getting used to its quarters, take the opportunity to observe its behaviour and learn some of its characteristics. Once your bird appears to be comfortable in the new environment, start to offer it pieces of food by hand to develop a bond between you. Young parrots and mynah birds often beg for food even though they are capable of feeding themselves.

MAKING CONTACT

Start the taming process by persuading your bird to step on to your hand. Slowly extend an index finger parallel with the perch where the bird is resting, then slide it beneath the bird's toes so that it becomes a replacement perch. With patience, you should find that your bird hops readily on to your hand in this way, so that you can then remove it from the cage and release it out into the room.

Hand-reared birds are quite used to perching on a hand and can usually be taken out of their cage with the minimum of fuss. When offering your hand, keep your fingers extended rather than folded together, as this is easier for the bird to grip. You may find that your bird's claws are sharp, as they have yet to be worn down naturally through perching. Try to avoid clipping them at this early stage, unless they are curling round at their tips and, instead, wear a thin glove for protection. Remove any shiny jewellery when handling a bird, as it is bound to attract its attention.

As you get to know your bird, gradually teach it to trust you by helping it out of the cage with an extended finger.

Flight restrictions

Before you introduce a routine of exercising your bird, you need to decide whether or not to clip the flight feathers on its wings. This protects birds from injury when they fly around the room, and should also stop your pet from escaping by flying off through an open window if it is frightened. Even so, you should bear in mind that a clipped bird will be less able to escape from would-be predators such as cats.

Never be tempted to tether a bird to a perch, as it will instinctively attempt to fly off when frightened. When it is abruptly jerked back by the restraining chain, the bird is likely to injure itself and become distressed.

Gaining confidence

When it has become used to its environment, a pet bird will often perch readily outside its cage. To accommodate this, some cages feature an external perch, which also allows any droppings to fall on to the cage floor below. Build up a routine with your bird where it spends set periods of the day out of its quarters. Before long, you are likely to find that your bird returns to its cage voluntarily.

Covering the cage

Birds should ideally receive a recommended maximum of 12 hours of light per day; excessive exposure to light is thought to increase moulting. If you intend to stay in the same room as your bird until late in the evening, it is best to place a loose cover over the cage, but make sure that the bird cannot catch its claws on the material.

TEACHING YOUR BIRD TO TALK

If you want your bird to talk, incorporate lessons into the taming process. It is essential to hold the bird's attention so that it listens to what you are saying. For this reason, audio training materials tend to be less effective than the bird being taught directly by a person. As a rule, most birds find it easier to learn from the high-pitched voice of a child or woman, and may take longer to learn when when trained by a man.

Patience is essential when teaching a bird to talk, as some species and even individuals appear to learn more slowly than others. For example, African grey parrots may not speak until they are six months old. It is also important that you do not spoil your bird's ability to talk by rushing the process.

WING-CLIPPING

Wing-clipping restricts but does not prevent a bird's flight, but it is pointless if your bird is tame and not easily alarmed. It is not a permanent handicap, since the cut feathers are moulted and replaced in time. When the wing is closed, the unclipped feathers mask the cut ones so that the bird's appearance is unaffected. Before undertaking wing-clipping, ask a vet to show you the correct procedure and always make sure that someone else helps you when you carry out this task.

inner feathers
left intact

feathers cut above
the shaft

outer two feathers
stay unclipped

Repetition

Repeat a chosen word or short phrase at intervals throughout the day but remember to keep each session brief enough to be certain of holding your bird's attention. Once the bird responds by repeating your words, you can add new material, but carry on repeating the existing vocabulary as well. By linking phrases together in this way, it is possible to teach birds to recite rhymes, for example, and to acquire a broad vocabulary.

Reciting a name and number

When establishing a vocabulary for your bird, it is a good idea to teach it to recite its personal details, even if the bird already carries this information on a micro-chip (see page 61). Each year, many tame birds escape through open windows or cage doors and are never reunited with their owners because they cannot be identified. Some parrots can fly 8km (5 miles) or more from their homes, so it is a good idea to teach your bird to repeat a contact address or telephone number, in case it is found. Do not despair if several days elapse before you receive any news – it may just be because your bird needs to recover from its ordeal before it starts to talk.

SHOWING BIRDS

If you intend to exhibit birds, your first move should be to join the national society for the type of bird in which you are interested. This organization is able to supply details of the current judging standards for classes, sets out what is considered to be the ideal representation of the breed, and can advise you on rings for your chicks.

What judges look for

The entries in a class are not judged directly against each other, but on how closely they conform to the perceived ideal of the breed. Points are awarded for specific features, such as coloration, markings, the type or appearance, and, in a few cases, even posture and movement. The breakdown of the points reflects the emphasis placed on particular criteria for the type concerned, but in all cases, the condition of the bird is vital. A moulting bird with correspondingly poor feathers cannot be expected to succeed in competitions.

Making progress

The various levels of competition start with beginners' classes and rise up to those for established champions. To make your way through the ranks, you need to gain a specified number of wins and experience. It is worth bearing in mind that a bird does not necessarily need to possess the qualities of a champion exhibitor for it to prove invaluable in a beginner's stud. Experienced exhibitors are usually keen to encourage newcomers and have a wealth of knowledge to share, so be prepared to listen to any guidance they may offer.

Parrots seem to find it easier to learn to talk from the high-pitched voices of women and children.

Preparing for the breeding season

Birds are only likely to breed if they are in good condition and are well established in an aviary. The settling-down period varies according to species and some, such as the large parrots, sometimes take several years to reach breeding condition.

REACHING BREEDING CONDITION

Most species nest in the summer months in temperate areas, although poicephalid parrots often prefer to nest during winter. The increase in daylight acts as a trigger for many birds, even in areas close to the equator where day length is relatively constant throughout the year. Birds housed indoors may be encouraged to respond in a similar way if over the course of several weeks you gradually increase the period of light exposure, or photoperiod, to 15 hours per day.

Boosting a bird's diet

Diet plays an important role in bringing a bird into breeding condition and breeders often feed their birds on special formulated foods just before the breeding season. Birds usually benefit from an increase in protein, and if they are on softbill diets, it also helps to increase the availability of live food.

By surgically sexing, a veterinarian is able to look directly at the bird's reproductive organs so he or she can check for abnormalities or signs of general illness.

SEXING BIRDS

With some bird species, it can be very easy to identify true breeding pairs and distinguishing between the sexes is straightforward due to obvious differences in size or plumage between the cock and hen. It is often said that hens may be slightly smaller or less colourful than their male counterparts, but these distinctions are not generally reliable as birds that originate from different areas may show a natural variation that is unrelated to their gender. For species that cannot be sexed visually, you will need to use a more reliable method of sexing.

Pelvic bone test

For many years, the pelvic bone test was the only alternative to visual sexing of birds. Unfortunately, it is of little value outside the relatively brief period when a hen bird is in egg-laying condition. Outside this period, or with immature birds, you will be unable to distinguish cocks from hens.

Holding the bird so that its back lies in the palm of your hand, you can feel its pelvic bones just above the vent. As hen birds reach breeding condition, the gap between these bones increases, as the ligaments slacken off to allow for the passage of the eggs. At this stage, it is possible to distinguish a hen bird in comparison with a cock bird.

Endoscopic or surgical sexing

The first laboratory method used to distinguish between the sexes was called faecal steroid analysis. This entailed testing for the presence of sex hormones in droppings but, unfortunately, did not prove reliable.

This was confirmed by surgical or endoscopic sexing, a test in which a vet inserts a probe called an endoscope, behind the last rib on the left-hand side of a bird's body. Depending on whether the vet can see the hen's oviduct or the cock's testes, the bird can be accurately sexed.

An added advantage of endoscopic sexing is that while looking at the reproductive system the vet can determine whether egg-laying is imminent, and identify any disorders of the reproductive tract. The drawbacks of this test, however, are that the bird has to be anaesthetized and that it cannot be performed on young birds. While anaesthetics for birds are now relatively safe, a slight unavoidable risk remains, especially if the bird being examined is overweight.

DNA TESTING

The rapid increases in DNA technology over recent years have meant that this genetic material - deoxyribonucleic acid nucleic acid - has now become most widely used for sexing purposes. There are none of the risks associated with endoscopic sexing and it has the further advantage that the gender of birds of any age can be determined in this way.

This can be especially valuable if you can identify cocks and hens with certainty as soon as they leave the nest. It also means that you can pair up cockatoos for example before they are mature, lessening the likelihood of aggressive encounters when they come into breeding condition. In the case of ring-necked parakeets (Psittacula krameri), you will be able to distinguish between 'splits' and pure green individuals (see page 94-95) in certain cases as soon as they fledge (or even before if required), which can be of great advantage when planning a breeding programme.

DNA sexing is also less stressful for the birds and more convenient for their keepers. In most cases now contour feathers can be used, with the DNA being extracted from the feather pulp at the bottom of the shaft, rather than blood. The sample is then placed in a special container and dispatched by courier to the laboratory.

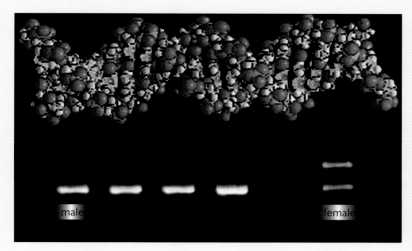

male   female

very fragile and this could cause problems in the nterpretation of results.

Keeping sample records

It is vital however, that you record carefully which bird was the source of a particular sample. If you do not note this information then you will be unable to interpret the results when they are received! It also helps if the birds are micro-chipped, so there can be no doubt about their gender in the future.

DNA sexing has also been used in another way to benefit bird keepers. Some laboratories store samples sent or them for security purposes. Should your bird be stolen in the future and then recovered, taking a fresh sample and comparing this with the one in storage will serve to confirm that these came from the same individual, if there is any dispute over ownership.

DNA fingerprinting of this type has also been used in courts to show that chicks allegedly bred from a particular pair were actually unrelated to them. Increasingly with the rare parrots, DNA monitoring of this type is likely to be used to prevent unintentional in-breeding of closely related individuals.

CONDITIONING FACTORS

Birds will only breed if they are in good condition and well established in their quarters. The length of time taken for birds to settle down depends partly on the species concerned, with larger parrots sometimes taking several years.

Daylight trigger

The majority of species will tend to nest in the summer months in temperate areas, although there can be some exceptions, with Poicephalus parrots sometimes preferring to nest during the winter.

It is the increasing day length which acts as a trigger for many species, even affecting those originating close to the equator, where day length is relatively constant throughout the year. Birds housed inside may respond in a similar way if the period of light exposure - called the photoperiod - is increased over the course of several weeks, typically up to 15 hours daily.

Boosting a bird's diet

The diet can also play a part, with an increase in the protein level appearing to be most significant. In the

Breeding equipment

By providing a choice of suitable nesting sites for your birds it is possible to stimulate breeding activity and encourage them to start nesting. Most birds can be bred in flights or aviaries, but exhibition birds are usually bred in specially designed breeding cages.

CHOOSING A NEST BOX

A good range of ready-made nest boxes is available from pet stores and bird suppliers. As a general guide, most birds prefer a small nest box relative to their size, with a correspondingly small entrance.

- Finch nest boxes may be sealed with a small entrance hole, or open-fronted, often with a small dowel perch just below the entrance for easy access.
- Nest boxes for parakeets and large parrots need to be robust enough to resist attack from their bills. They should be made from plywood of at least 1.25cm (½in) in thickness and joined with screws rather than nails, so that the box can be dismantled for cleaning or repair.

- Parakeets prefer the deeper type of nest box, often described as a 'grandfather clock'. Running down the inside of the box is a ladder made from a strip of wire mesh, with carefully trimmed ends to prevent any injury to the bird. When siting the nest box check that the ladder is secured inside the box, so that it cannot be knocked over and damage any eggs or chicks.

Access to the nest box is important for monitoring progress, so choose one with a hinged or sliding lid. Alternatively, some nest boxes incorporate a separate side inspection hatch that enables you to look inside with minimum disturbance. This is especially useful for checking on parrots as they can become aggressive when defending their nest.

Siting a nest box

Nest boxes need to be properly supported so that they are able to take the weight of the resident birds. Small nest boxes, such as those used by finches, and canary

Make sure that any nest box or other nesting site is well constructed and suits the size of your birds. Nest pans are used by canary hens as bases for their nests. Some finches may prefer to use wicker nesting baskets. The wire supports at the back of these can be slipped on to the fronts of breeding cages or over aviary mesh. They can also be held in place by netting staples driven into the back of wooden flights.

grandfather clock-type nest box

budgerigar breeding box

woven nest pan

plastic nest pan with felt liner

open-fronted nest box for finches or softbills

domed nesting basket for finches

nesting basket for finches or softbills

NESTING BASICS

Some birds, such as finches and softbills, prefer to build their own nests and require special nesting material. Choose safe, bird-friendly materials offered for sale at pet stores and bird suppliers, and provide relatively small amounts at a time so that it does not become soiled. Special dispensers are available to enable birds to take what they need.

Spaghnum moss, popular with softbills, is sold in florists, and thin twigs can be picked up in gardens. Lovebirds and hanging parrots will use branches and fresh leaves. Provide large parrots with thin wooden battening on the floor of their nest box, which they can whittle away to form a nest. Supply budgerigars with wooden concaves on which to lay their eggs.

To ensure canary eggs all hatch at the same time, replace each egg with a dummy as it is laid, then put all the real eggs back together.

dummy canary eggs

strands of nesting material

coconut fibre

fibrous nesting material

nesting material in holder

felt liner for nest pan

---

nest pans can be screwed directly to the framework of the aviary. Large boxes are best supported below by L-shaped brackets attached firmly to the aviary framework. Make sure that the fixing screws do not penetrate the base of the box as they might damage any eggs.

USING A BREEDING CAGE

Exhibitors prefer to breed their birds in breeding cages rather than letting them pair at random in an aviary. You can either buy a ready-made cage or construct your own breeding cage – a less-expensive option that can be quite simple to perform, thanks to the range of special cage fronts that are available from suppliers.

Making a breeding cage

When calculating the size of your cage, add 2.5–5cm (1–2in) to the size of the cage front. This allows room for a sliding tray beneath the cage as well as an external wooden framework. If you simply use the height of the cage front as your template, the resulting cage will be too low for the birds. Use oil-tempered hardboard (or light plywood

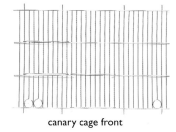

canary cage front

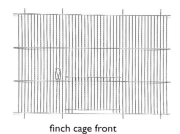

finch cage front

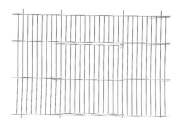

budgerigar cage front

for budgerigars) for the box unit. The smooth side should form the inner face of the cage, which you should attach to an outer wooden framework using panel pins. Before fixing the cage front, paint the cage interior with white emulsion to lighten it up. When it is dry, fix the cage front on with screws so that it can be dismantled for cleaning at the end of the breeding season.

Fitting a perch

Cut a natural branch or piece of dowel to the width of the cage, to provide perching. Glue or pin the perch firmly in position inside the cage, siting it in such a way that birds can turn around easily without catching their tails. Remember that if the perch is unstable, pairs might be unable to mate properly.

Cage fronts are available in a range of sizes and are specifically designed for budgerigars, finches, and canaries. The principal difference is in the bar spacing. Always select a cage front to suit the size of your birds, as finch chicks may become caught in widely spaced bars.

Potential breeding problems

However carefully you might prepare for the breeding season, there is no guarantee that you will have successful results, especially with birds that are nesting for the first time. You will need to spend a lot of time watching your birds at all stages of breeding, from mating, through egg-laying, to checking on chicks inside the nest boxes. If you know your birds, you will be better placed to detect any problems at an early stage.

EGG-BINDING

Hens, particularly young hens laying for the first time and old birds at the end of their reproductive lives, commonly suffer from egg-binding, in which an egg becomes lodged in the reproductive tract. The egg's soft rubbery shell is often thought to be the cause of the problem, but it is more often due to the action of the muscles in this part of the reproductive tract. Calcium plays a vital role in muscular contraction, to the extent that a deficiency may well prevent the hen from being able to expel an egg from her body.

What to do about egg-binding

When the hens are likely to be laying, look into the aviary at least twice a day so you will notice any bird that might look poorly. The signs of egg-binding are easy to recognize, and an afflicted bird will have ruffled plumage and look unsteady on its feet. Once you have identified the symptoms transfer the bird from the

CANDLING

Many eggs fail to hatch simply because they were never fertilized. A technique known as candling is used to determined the state of an egg. At a fairly advanced stage in the incubation hold the egg against a strong source of light. If you can see the light through the egg, it is described as being 'clear', meaning that it is infertile. A fertile egg will appear opaque.

fertile egg

aviary to a warm place and dose it with a soluble calcium supplement. Within a short space of time this can directly assist the passage of the egg by acting as a muscle tonic. You could also try lubricating the vent to manipulate the egg free, but take great care not to rupture the egg as this could lead to infection. If the supplement fails to help the hen, prompt veterinary

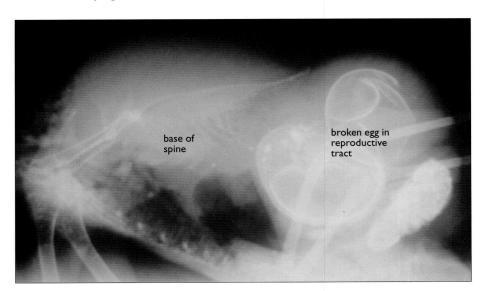

base of spine

broken egg in reproductive tract

If you suspect a hen of suffering from egg-binding you should be able to feel the egg as a slight swelling between her legs, but if it is trapped at a higher point in the reproductive tract, it may be necessary to organize an X-ray. This radiograph shows two retained eggs, one of which has broken. A ruptured egg could trigger peritonitis in the bird with potentially fatal results. Great care must therefore be taken when handling a bird with egg-binding.

attention is essential. An injection of calcium borogluconate may be required, or, in more extreme cases, even surgery. Hens can make a good recovery, from surgery of this type, and, after a few months' convalescence, can breed again.

INFERTILE EGGS

There are a number of reasons why eggs may be infertile. Infertility can often be linked to the age of a bird and may just indicate that a cock bird is too young to breed successfully. This problem often arises when mating large parrots, as you cannot be certain that a cock bird is mature unless it has been examined with an endoscope.

Difficulties in mating

Infertile eggs often result from unsuccessful mating – even something as simple as a loose perch can prevent a pair from completing the act successfully. Physical barriers such as dense plumage might also be to blame for unsuccessful mating. For this reason, canary breeders often trim the vent area of heavily feathered birds before putting them in their breeding quarters.

Sometimes, a hen budgerigar is so keen to start laying immediately that she disappears into the nest box without giving the cock bird an opportunity to mate with her. To prevent this from happening, when the pair are first placed in the breeding cage, you might want to block off the entrance to the nest box for a few days, to increase the chance of a successful mating.

CHICKS FALLING FROM NEST

Once chicks have hatched, the need for constant observation becomes essential, as the nestlings can inadvertently be pulled out of the nest by adult birds. If a newly hatched chick is lying across the foot of the hen when she suddenly moves off to feed, then the chick is likely to be flipped out of the nest and onto the floor of the breeding cage. Depending on the temperature, the chick may survive on the floor for several hours, but it is unlikely to survive overnight, as it will not have been fed during this period. Try to check the cages carefully at least twice every day, preferably in the morning and evening to make sure that you see any distressed chicks.

What to do with a fallen chick

If you come across a chick that has clearly fallen from the nest, do not immediately give up hope even if it appears to be dead. Instead, hold the bird gently between the cupped palms of your hands for several

CALCIUM SUPPLEMENTS

Birds, particularly hens, need extra calcium, which is vital for the production of strong, healthy egg shells. Calcium-rich cuttlefish bone is the traditional means of supplementing the diet of seed-eating birds. Offer grated pieces to small birds, such as finches, which may find it difficult to nibble the bone.

Soluble calcium supplements, which are added to drinking water, can provide a very effective means of supplementing a bird's calcium intake in the breeding season. Follow the supplier's instructions for their use carefully, though, because overdosing a bird is likely to have harmful consequences.

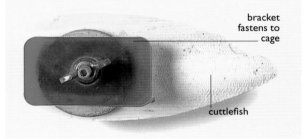

bracket fastens to cage

cuttlefish

minutes to warm it up. If you are fortunate enough to feel it wriggle, continue warming it for a little longer before placing it back under the hen. The chick is likely to recover uneventfully from its ordeal, but it is a good idea to check on its progress the next day, encouraging the hen off the nest for this purpose.

Problems with ill-fitting concaves

Concaves should fit snugly inside a nest box without leaving any gap between the sides. Otherwise, this can prove to be a death trap for young chicks that are unlucky enough to be rolled out as their parents move to and from the nest. Once the chicks become trapped at the bottom of the nest box they remain largely out of sight until the nest is checked carefully and the nestlings are counted individually. Chicks huddle closely together on the concave, making it very easy to miss a nestling, especially if it is one of the smaller offspring in a brood.

Resolving the problem

Although a fallen chick can be picked up, you should aim to prevent accidents like this from happening again. Construct a frame for the concave, or buy a concave that fits snugly. As a short-term measure, you can fill in the gaps around the concave with bird sand.

Rearing and feeding the chicks

Incubating the eggs and raising a brood of hungry chicks is a demanding task for adult birds and they need your help, especially in meeting the chicks' nutritional demands. In some instances, breeders may decide to incubate the eggs artificially and hand-rear chicks rather than leaving it to the parents.

ARTIFICIAL INCUBATION

A good selection of small-scale incubators suitable for hatching parrot eggs is available from specialist outlets. If you decide to hatch eggs in this way, you may find it useful to choose a machine that features automatic turning and a suitable grid for the eggs. This avoids the need to open the incubator several times each day, and turn the eggs by hand.

Place the incubator on a level surface, preferably away from any windows and out of direct sunlight, which could cause undesirable fluctuations in temperature and affect the number of eggs that hatch.

The ideal incubation temperature should be between 36.9 and 37.5°C (98.5 and 99.5°F), which can easily be maintained in a modern incubator. The other important factor is the relative humidity, which must remain constant to prevent the eggs from dehydrating. Eggs lose water throughout incubation, so always check that the water reservoir in the incubator is topped up.

HELPING BREEDING PAIRS

You will need to provide breeding pairs with suitable rearing foods to ensure the rapid growth of their chicks. At this time, many birds, even seed-eaters, require animal protein and invertebrates, such as crickets. You will need to supply insectivorous birds with a supply of suitably sized live food (see pages 88–9). If you notice a sudden fall-off in food consumption, inspect the nest to discover the root of the problem.

While chicks are unlikely to be reared successfully if the diet of the adult birds is deficient, young birds may be neglected as a result of problems that are quite unrelated to diet. One common cause is when the nest has suffered from heavy interference at the start of the breeding period. Try to restrain your curiosity during this sensitive time, only glimpsing in the nest when the adult birds have left it momentarily.

First-time pairs of large parrots, such as macaws, often fail to master their feeding technique properly. Cockatoos, in particular, are vulnerable to losing one of their chicks for this reason, as the dominant chick obtains more food than its sibling and grows faster. Before long, the smaller chick has to fight to obtain any food, and becomes progressively weaker. If you notice this happening in the nest, remove the smaller chick for supplementary feeds taking care not to attract the wrath of the adult bird, which may become aggressive.

A young budgerigar chick emerges from the nest box for the first time.

HAND-REARING CHICKS

The need to hand-rear a chick often arises in an emergency, so make sure that you have the necessary equipment ready during the breeding season. Hand-rearing itself has become much easier, thanks to the availability of specially formulated rearing foods. If possible, choose a brand that includes a probiotic to compensate for the absence of beneficial bacteria to line the gut. This would normally be passed on from the adult birds to their offspring to improve their resistance to infection. Cleanliness is essential when you are hand-rearing birds. Using a detergent, wash and rinse all feeding implements and equipment thoroughly after each feed and throw away any unused food.

Temperature

It is vital to keep the chicks warm, at a steady temperature of 38–40°C (100–105°F) for recently hatched chicks. A thermostatically controlled brooder unit is ideal for this purpose, but a light bulb hung over the chick's quarters provides an effective alternative in an emergency. Choose a dull light if possible, even though the chick's eyes may be closed, and check the temperature regularly. As the chick grows, the temperature in its quarters should be gradually reduced to room temperature.

Feeding a chick

The number of feeds required depends on the age of the chick, and the species concerned. Newly hatched chicks may need feeding every two hours at first, with a slightly longer gap overnight. This interval between feeds gradually lengthens to about four hours. As a guide to the bird's hunger, check the appearance of the crop at the base of the neck, and try not to let it fall completely slack – a clear sign that the chick is hungry.

Although it is possible to use a small syringe (with the needle removed) for hand-feeding chicks, a teaspoon with slightly bent edges is a better option (see page 87). Using a syringe involves forcing the food through the nozzle and you risk choking the chick. With a teaspoon, however, the young bird can feed at its own pace. Always wipe the chick's bill after each feed. If any food is allowed to stick and harden on the relatively soft tissue in this area, it is likely to result in permanent malformation.

Weight loss at the weaning stage is quite normal, as the chick will lose interest in the food that you are offering. Place alternative sources of food, together with drinking water, within reach of the chick so that it can start to eat on its own.

WARNING

Birds with powerful bills, such as most parrots, frequently nibble at the skin of their legs, and may toy with their rings. For this reason, it is better to use strong stainless-steel bands on these birds, as aluminium rings are too flimsy. Check the ring regularly for signs of interference, as it may start to exert pressure on the lower leg causing swelling and it may, if left, disrupt the the blood supply.

RINGING BIRDS

Some species are required by law to wear rings, and they can be especially significant for exhibition birds. Order closed-rings of a suitable size in advance, so that they are ready to be fitted within the first week after hatching. Carry out ringing in a good light, and preferably on a level surface. Hold the leg carefully, making sure that the chick cannot fall, then clasp the longest three toes together and pass the ring up to the ball of the foot. Keeping the short rear toe parallel with the upper part of the leg, slide the ring over the top then free the rear toe, using a blunt match stick if necessary to carry out this manoeuvre. If the chick is older than a week or two since its hatching, it might not be possible to pass the ring freely over the foot. However, if you attempt to ring the bird too early, the band may simply slide off the foot.

Place the chicks back in the nest as soon as possible after banding them. Some breeders advocate wiping some nest dirt over the rings, to make them less conspicuous. In species that instinctively clean their nests, this reduces the risk of the adult bird, ejecting its chick, because of the foreign body on its leg.

KEEPING BREEDING RECORDS

There is little point in banding the birds if you do not keep records of your stock, enabling you to identify the origins of an individual. Keeping breeding records is particularly important for young chicks, although you should also record the numbers of purchased birds that are already rung in a stock register. Breeders often use a card index system during the breeding season. They attach a card to the outside of each nest box in the bird room and note when the pair were introduced; when laying occurred; the numbers of eggs; when the chicks hatched; and how many offspring were successfully reared, placing the ring numbers alongside a description of each one. This information can then be transferred to a stock register.

Weaning chicks

cock

The weaning period, when chicks learn to become dependent and feed themselves, can be a hazardous time for young birds and they often become victims of attack from adult birds. Your encouragement and watchful eye at this crucial stage will help steer them through to maturity.

ATTACKS ON PLUMAGE

Savage assaults on the plumage of chicks are common among budgerigars, lutino cockatiels, and peach-faced lovebirds. Such attacks are carried out by adult birds who, surprisingly, resume rearing the chicks without further problems. It is difficult to identify whether the hen or the cock bird is responsible for the attacks, but once this type of feather-plucking has occurred, the pair is likely to attack subsequent broods in a similar way.

Chicks appear to be most vulnerable in the period from when the feathers start to emerge to when they unfurl. It may be that adult birds start to preen their offspring too soon, before the feathers are ready to emerge properly, and so pull out the plumage in frustration. Plucking is confined mainly to the nape of the neck and on the upper part of the wings – areas that the chick is unable to reach by itself.

Few chicks suffer any lasting physical injury from these incidents, although they often tend to be more nervous than those that have not experienced such attacks. The remainder of their plumage grows normally, and they usually leave the nest box with the start of new feathering evident in the plucked areas.

Male plum-headed parakeets (**Psittacula cyanocephala**) *usually assume the task of feeding the offspring when they emerge from the nest. Once the chicks are able to feed themselves they can be removed from their parents.*

What can you do?

By the time you have discovered chicks that have lost their feathers, the bleeding will have ceased. In the following two or three days, bruising of the surrounding skin becomes apparent but subsides in due course. Any damage to the underlying skin is rare. If they have been severely plucked, cockatiels and other birds bred in flights are likely to become chilled during bad weather. Provided that the birds are already feeding themselves, bring them indoors to recover.

Special sprays have recently become available to help prevent attacks on plumage. These are applied to the back and wings just before the chicks start to feather up, but their effectiveness is not proven.

HAZARDS IN FLEDGING

Young birds are very sensitive during fledging and can easily be upset. While you can try to deter unwelcome visitors such as cats from prowling around the aviary and inducing panic, natural disturbances such as thunder and lightning are beyond your control.

Young chicks can quickly become waterlogged in heavy rain, especially if the nest is sited in the path of rain running off the roof and into the flight itself.

FOSTERING

If you have a pair of adult birds that are known to attack the plumage of chicks, you may be able to foster their eggs to another nest. For the transfer to be successful, make sure that eggs in the foster nest were laid at approximately the same time, so that the chicks are of a similar age when they hatch. With a pencil, mark the shells of eggs being transferred so you can identify the resulting chicks.

Unfortunately, fostering may not provide a long-term solution to the problem of attacks on plumage, since the young birds may themselves develop into feather-pluckers when they have chicks. It might be better, therefore, simply to sell the chicks as pets, rather than keeping them for breeding purposes.

chick

hen

For this reason, guttering is essential in an aviary and needs to be kept in good condition. Check the gutters regularly for any blockages that can cause torrents of water that are likely to soak the birds and their nests.

Many chicks leave the nest before they are able to fly properly and risk becoming waterlogged in heavily planted enclosures. Make sure that you can account for all your newly fledged chicks as dusk approaches, to be certain that they have chosen a safe roosting site. This danger passes within a week or so.

'Night fright'

Most fatalities occur at night, when young birds are unable to make their way to a perch. Finding themselves in difficulty, the birds start to fly around the area wildly and upset their companions. This type of panic is often described as 'night fright' and usually results in one or more fatalities (see pages 108–9).

If you are unfortunate enough to come across dead chicks on the floor of the aviary one morning, look carefully for signs of injury on the head and cere, which tend to indicate night fright. However, to be certain of the cause of death, you may wish to arrange for an autopsy to be carried out by your vet.

Intestinal worms

Recently fledged Australian parakeets commonly suffer from intestinal worms. They acquire the infective eggs from pecking around in nest litter contaminated by adult birds and unfortunately in young birds, even a relatively light burden of these parasites can have fatal consequences. Treatment is possible (see page 106) if the condition is recognized in time.

Flying into the aviary mesh

Many Australian parakeets are particularly nervous when fledging and might attempt to fly through the aviary mesh. One of the best ways of making sure that a young bird does not harm itself in this way is to train non-poisonous annuals, such as climbing nasturtiums (*Tropaeolum majus*), up the aviary mesh (see page 52). These plants grow rapidly, even in poor soil, and are easily grown from seed. They can create attractive cover at the far end of a flight, which is the main area of danger, and their leaves are safe for birds to nibble on. An alternative type of cover can be made by fitting a sheet of dark plastic across a wooden framework, which can then be screwed on to the outside of the aviary framework.

Aggressive parents

Some adult pairs, notably Australian parakeets and parrotlets, are very aggressive towards their offspring. Once you are certain that the fledglings are able to feed on their own, transfer them to separate accommodation to avoid any risk of them being attacked by adult birds.

To encourage young birds to start feeding on their own, provide soaked seed and fruit. They will tend to toy with their food and you will need to clean up often.

Breeding for colour

All the characteristics of an individual bird, including its coloration, are encoded on genes. These are located on structures called chromosomes which are present in the nucleus of every living cell in the body. At fertilization, one set of chromosomes from each parent is brought together and, in this way, genes are passed from one generation to the next.

Genes combine at random making it impossible to be sure which characteristics will appear in a new bird. You can, however, assess the possible combinations and arrive at a set of predictions for a pairing. These calculations are based on the genetic studies of Gregor Mendel (1822–84), an Austrian monk who noted how specific characteristics were passed down generations.

MUTATIONS

Most colour mutations, including blues and yellows, are autosomal, as are recessive pieds in budgerigars. The term 'autosomal' indicates that the genes are located not on sex chromosomes but on other chromosomes, which are described collectively as autosomes.

Sex-linked

The best known examples of sex-linked mutations are the lutino and cinnamon colours, which are now common in many species, including budgerigars, peach-faced lovebirds, and Indian ring-necked parakeets, and the pearl in cockatiels. Sex-linked recessive mutations affect the pair of sex chromosomes, which determine a bird's gender. These are uneven in length in hen birds, so that hens bred from sex-linked pairings cannot be split for colour mutation although they may still carry a hidden autosomal feature. The key difference when pairing up birds of a sex-linked mutation is to opt for a mutation cock bird to pair with a normal hen, rather than vice-versa, to produce mutation offspring that are all be hens in the first (or F1) generation. The likely breeding results for sex-linked pairings are:

- **Green cock x lutino hen**
  50% green/lutino cocks; 50% green hens
- **Green/lutino cock x lutino hen**
  25% green/lutino cocks; 25% lutino cocks; 25% lutino hens; 25% green hens
- **Lutino cock x lutino hen**
  50% lutino cocks; 50% lutino hens
- **Lutino cock x green hen**
  50% green/lutino cocks; 50% lutino hens

Dominant type

Less commonly, some mutations such as the spangle form of the budgerigar, have proved to be dominant to the normal form, and it has been possible to breed them quite rapidly. In these cases, the genetic make-up is effectively reversed, so that birds can be either single factor (sf) or double factor (df), depending on whether one or both genes are affected. It is usually impossible to distinguish between these forms in Australian dominant pied budgerigars, although a distinct difference in coloration is apparent in the silver forms of the cockatiel and the spangle. When just one chromosome is affected in dark-factor mutations (see page 36), a single dark-factor bird results, while the double dark-factor is produced when two factors are present. Mating two single-factor birds together should produce offspring of both shades, as well as normals. The likely breeding results for dark-factor pairings are:

- **Olive (df) x light green**
  100% dark green (sf)
- **Olive (df) x dark green (sf)**
  50% dark green (sf); 50% olive (df)
- **Olive (df) x olive (df)**
  100% olive (df)
- **Dark green (sf) x dark green (sf)**
  25% light green; 50% dark green (sf); 25% olive (df)
- **Dark green (sf) x light green**
  50% dark green (sf); 50% light green

Crested

Several species, including the Bengalese and zebra finches, can be bred in crested forms. However, even though this is a dominant mutation, pairings are slightly different because of the presence of a lethal factor associated with the double-factor form, whereby chicks either do not hatch at all or die soon after hatching. Lethal factors are fortunately rare in bird breeding. The only other case of this type involves the blue mutation of the splendid grass parakeet, which unlike crested mutations, is an autosomal recessive mutation. Hence, crested birds (excluding those that occur naturally in crested form) should be paired with non-crested birds known as plainheads. The likely breeding results for crested pairings are:

- **Crested (sf) x normal**
  50% crested (sf); 50% normal

COLOUR EXPECTATIONS FOR SPLIT BIRDS

Where opposing genes or chromosomes are present, one of them emerges as dominant and can mask the other. For example, if you pair a light-green with a sky-blue budgerigar only light-green offspring are produced as the light-green colour is dominant. Although it is not visible in the chick's appearance (phenotype), the sky-blue characteristic in its genetic make-up (genotype) is still retained or 'carried'. Such birds are described as split (heterozygous) — indicated in shorthand by an oblique line placed after the dominant feature — and are indistinguishable in colour from ordinary light green. If this split bird is paired with a budgerigar of a similar genotype or a pure sky-blue, you can expect some sky-blue offspring in this second generation of birds.

This diagram, known as the Punnett Square system, shows how it is possible to predict the likely outcome from pairings. All the genetic characteristics of the birds are separated out at right angles to each other, and then the chart is filled in, to show the likely colour expectancies of the offspring, based on the various possible combinations of the genes. In this example, the pair are both light-green budgerigars split for sky-blue, which means that they are light green in appearance but carry the sky-blue gene.

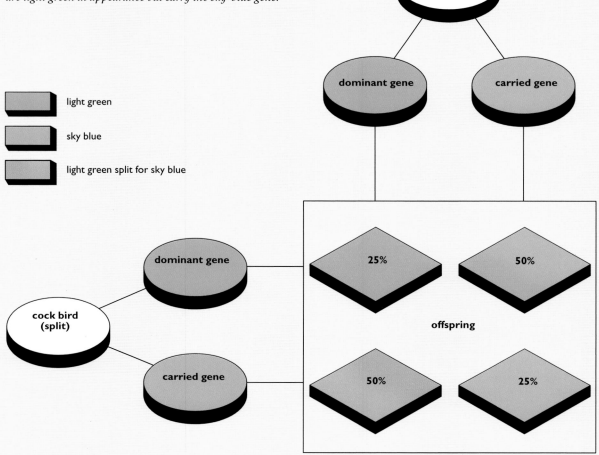

light green

sky blue

light green split for sky blue

Foods and feeding

A balanced diet is essential for pet and aviary birds, especially during breeding and the moult, when their nutritional requirements often change. It may take a while to establish which foods your birds prefer, especially at the weaning stage, but time spent making dietary changes is rewarded with healthy-looking birds.

Nutrition

Birds are often grouped according to whether they are seed-eaters or softbills. Yet this is too simplistic as many finches, though indeed seed-eaters, will also take a wide variety of other foods. The term softbill, which describes all non-seed eating birds, from – seagulls to hummingbirds – is even less meaningful.

TYPES OF SEED
Seeds can be divided into two categories, based on their nutritional value. Cereals, such as canary seed, millets, and groats are characterized by a relatively high level of carbohydrate and low amount of fat and protein. This profile is reversed in oil-based seeds, such as red rape, sunflower, hemp, and perilla, which have a high proportion of fat and protein, but a low carbohydrate content. Perilla is a general conditioner for birds, and helps them through the moult, while liberal servings of hemp help birds to maintain their body temperature when housed outdoors in winter.

Seeds alone do not offer a balanced diet, as they are generally low in vital ingredients such as vitamin A and calcium. They also lack protein, notably lysine, which is needed for good plumage. Try to offer a food with a higher protein content to ensure healthy feathering, especially during the moult, and select a mixture of seeds to compensate for any known deficiencies in one particular type, although growing conditions can cause variation in their nutritional value. When choosing seeds, therefore, try to obtain a blend of products from more than one country of origin.

Sourcing seeds
Buying seed from a specialist merchant should guarantee a fresh, clean supply of food, but do not hesitate to reject any dusty goods, as these are

FOOD REQUIREMENTS

A bird's diet should comprise three basic components: carbohydrates and fat for energy, protein for growth, and vitamins and minerals to protect the body against illness and maintain general good health.

Reputable seed suppliers offer only peanuts that have been screened to make sure that they are not contaminated with aflatoxins. These deadly fungal toxins can cause irreversible liver damage to birds and are fatal. It is usually impossible to detect any visual difference between contaminated peanuts and those that are safe, so you must be confident that you are buying them from a reliable source.

---

potentially dangerous to birds. Specialist stockists usually offer a wide range of ready-made seed mixes that are specially formulated to suit a particular type of bird. An established seed merchant should also be able to supply tonic seeds, such as niger and blue maw seed, which are ideal for weaning canaries, and can be sprinkled over soft food.

Keeping seed

Seeds have a limited shelf life, and need to be stored in clean, dry surroundings. Their nutritional value declines over a period of time, so make sure that you always use your stock in rotation, rather than simply topping up your existing supply with new seed.

Store the food in sealed containers to prevent contamination by rodents, which can spread diseases such as yersiniosis (see pages 100–1) and salmonellosis. Once introduced, these bacterial infections spread quickly and can cause heavy losses in an aviary.

Check your stocks of seed regularly for signs of fodder mites. These are hard to spot but the easiest way of detecting their presence is to run a sample of seed through your hand and sniff it. When present, fodder mites make the seed slightly sticky, and give it a distinctive sickly smell.

COMPLETE DIETS

Complete foods are used mostly for parrots, although similar diets are available for smaller birds, such as finches and canaries. As with seed, store them in a dry place and do not use them after their expiry date as their vitamin content is likely to be adversely affected. Although these foods appear to be quite expensive when compared with seed, very little goes to waste. As the name suggests, complete diets contain all the vitamins and minerals necessary to birds, so you do not need to use a supplement in their diet. Continue to offer fresh items, such as fruit, however, and provide enough water as they are likely to drink more on a dry diet.

Introducing new foods

At first, your bird may be reluctant to sample a complete food, so try adding just a small quantity of it to the existing diet. As the bird comes to accept the food, you can gradually increase the amount given, reducing the seed content of the diet at the same time.

It is much simpler to use complete foods with young hand-reared birds as they can be weaned on to this type of diet before they establish feeding preferences. It is particularly important to introduce a variety of food to young parrots, as they are resistant to changes in their diet when they become adults.

Pellets and crumbles

Softbills will usually take pellets straight from the packet in a separate container. However, if they reject them, soak the pellets to improve their palatability and mix them in with other food. Discard the remains of any uneaten food daily to prevent it turning mouldy.

Smaller 'crumbles' are available for finches and help to compensate for the inadequacies of a seed-based diet. For maximum benefit, the birds should be fed exclusively on crumbles rather than seed.

Branded packets of seed tend to be more expensive than loose seed, but the quality is likely to be better since it will probably be free from dust. Depending on the hygiene of the supplier's premises, some loose seed is also clean, but there is always a greater chance that it has been contaminated by dust, moisture, or rodents.

striped sunflower

white millet

rape

plain canary

hemp

safflower

black sunflower

complete food

red millet

groats

pine nuts

Nectars and soft foods

Some birds, mainly softbills such as hummingbirds and tanagers, but even some parrots, feed on nectar, which is a sugary liquid that is rapidly absorbed into the body. It is also sometimes given as a tonic to revive softbills after a journey. Other softbills eat soft foods, which are ready-made preparations designed to provide the birds with a balanced diet.

NECTAR

It is vital to choose the right type of nectar food for your birds. Nectar intended for lories is unlikely to keep many of the smaller nectar-eaters in peak condition. Nectar products contain a carefully balanced range of vitamins and minerals, and do not need to be given with a supplement. They can generally be obtained from large pet stores or specialist suppliers. Dry nectar, which can be sprinkled over fruit, is taken readily by most lories and lorikeets, but it should not be used exclusively in place of a nectar solution.

Choosing a drinker

A range of nectar drinkers is available to suit the feeding habits of individual species. For example, hummingbirds use tubes made of tinted glass or plastic. These have long, thin nozzles with red markings around their bases to attract the birds to feed. Never offer nectar in open pots as the birds often end up with sticky plumage, and may even try to bathe in the pot.

Hygiene is vital when keeping nectivores, as their food provides an ideal environment for the growth of microbes. Use a bottle brush and washing-up

Birds such as hummingbirds use special drinkers. The tip of the spout is red to attract birds and encourage them to drink.

liquid for cleaning drinkers, and keep at least one spare set in case of breakages. This also allows one or more drinkers to be soaked in a sterilizing solution overnight, but remember to rinse the sterilized bottles before use. While glass tubes are easily broken, and leak if not correctly stoppered, they can be cleaned thoroughly and are less susceptible to scratching than plastic.

Preparing feeds

Always prepare fresh nectar for each feed (following the manufacturer's instructions), rather than leaving a supply in the fridge and warming it up again when required. Replace nectar solutions every 24 hours, and possibly twice a day when the weather is hot, as contaminated food can give rise to a fatal diarrhoea. Avoid introducing a sudden change in nectar solution,

Preparing nectar
Make up the right strength of solution, using a measuring jug. Do not use boiling water as it is likely to burn the bird's tongue if it feeds before the solution has cooled.

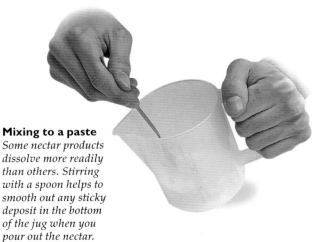

Mixing to a paste
Some nectar products dissolve more readily than others. Stirring with a spoon helps to smooth out any sticky deposit in the bottom of the jug when you pour out the nectar.

especially if your birds are new. Keep to the diet that they have been used to, making changes gradually after a fortnight or so. This should help to prevent any potentially fatal digestive upset.

SOFT FOODS

A wide range of soft foods is available for softbills, from general-purpose to insectivorous diets. Soft foods made for budgerigars and parakeets have a higher protein content than seed, which makes them especially valuable during the moult.

Virtually all soft foods can be fed straight from the packet, but if water is required, add a little at a time, sufficient to moisten rather than drench the food. Some birds are reluctant to eat soft food in this form, or are messy eaters and tend to waste the food. In such cases, add some fruit to the soft food and mix them together so that the fruit becomes coated with the food. This way of serving soft food is also useful for ensuring that your birds are receiving sufficient nutrients. Always keep the packet sealed to prevent the food from drying out, or store the food in a airtight container. If you buy food in bulk quantities, make sure that you note down the expiry date.

Iron-related problems

A major advance in softbill foods in recent years has been the introduction of low-iron softbill diets. These help to prevent iron storage disease, which is common in fruit-eating softbills, such as toucans and tanagers. An affected bird will have difficulty in flying, flutter to the ground, and will tend to spend longer at the food pot than normal. If, on examining the bird more closely, you discover that it also has a swollen abdomen, treatment may prove to be difficult. To prevent the onset of this condition, consult your vet for advice on a suitable low-iron soft food and restrict the amount of dry fruit in the bird's diet.

EGG FOODS

Egg foods tend to be used mainly in the breeding season as a rearing food, but there is no reason why they cannot be fed at other times of the year, such as during the moult when the additional protein content can be valuable. Avoid feeding red-factor canaries with egg food during the moult, however, as the lutein in the egg yolk is likely to colour the new plumage orange rather than red. Although few breeders prepare their own egg foods nowadays, some commercial foods include the traditional ingredients of dandelion and shepherd's purse.

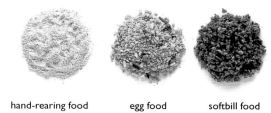

hand-rearing food   egg food   softbill food

Softbill foods comprise a mixture of cereals and insects, ground down into a soft powder. Ready prepared egg and hand-rearing foods are important when raising chicks.

HAND-REARING FOODS

As well as offering a balanced diet, hand-rearing foods have greatly simplified the process of raising chicks. They have also helped to eliminate ailments such as 'greenstick' fractures, which were caused by home-made foods that lacked sufficient nutrition.

Although these foods do not need vitamin or mineral supplements, the addition of a probiotic may be advisable to reduce the likelihood of enteric ailments and to assist the bird's rate of growth. It is worth remembering that growth rates may be slightly higher using these specialist foods.

As the chicks mature, it may be possible to wean them on to an equivalent complete diet, which makes the change-over period less traumatic.

HAND-FEEDING CHICKS

The task of hand-feeding chicks should not be rushed (see page 79). Mix the food fresh for each feed, making sure that it is warm enough – around 40°C (105°F). Use different feeding utensils for each batch of chicks.

Live foods

In the wild, birds do not eat the same diet throughout the year. Many birds, such as finches, which normally feed on seeds for most of the year, develop a strong instinct to feed on live foods such as insects or insect larvae during the breeding season, once their offspring have hatched. The raised level of protein that these foods provide in their diet helps them to sustain the rapid growth of their chicks.

PROVIDING LIVE FOOD

During the rearing period it is vital that you maintain the supply of live food for your birds, otherwise you run the risk of the chicks being abandoned by their parents. There are many commercial suppliers and it is advisable to place a regular standing order with a reliable company to ensure you never run short. Although soft foods (see page 87) are not a substitute for live foods, it is always a good idea to offer these to the fledglings during the rearing period thus reducing their dependence on the live foods.

It is better to provide live food in two or three batches during the day, rather than in one large amount in the morning. Remember to keep the food trough under a covered part of the aviary so that it does not become waterlogged by rain.

Crickets

many bird-keepers use crickets, which are available in a range of sizes to suit your bird's appetite. They are more nutritional than mealworms, with, on average 13 per cent fat and 73 per cent protein, although their calcium content is poor. Their advantage over other live food is that they can be treated with a powdered supplement to compensate for this.

crickets

waxworms

small
mealworms

standard mealworms

Live foods can be ordered from a reputable supplier. Always choose a food that is appropriate for the size and type of bird.

Simply sprinkle the required amount of supplement powder over the crickets before giving them to the birds. Without this addition, the relatively low level of calcium in their diet means that the birds will soon suffer from a calcium deficiency, which may produce a high percentage of soft-shelled eggs and cause egg-binding in egg-laying hens.

Crickets feed on cereals and grass, and can be kept in a hooded aquarium with a scrunched-up newspaper in which to hide, and a wet sponge for water.

You will normally be able to persuade small birds to take hatchling crickets without much difficulty, particularly if the crickets are first chilled in the fridge to slow their activity. It can help to place the crickets in a deep-sided trough so the birds can fly down and catch them without difficulty. It also prevents crickets from becoming lost in the aviary, particularly in a planted flight.

Mealworms

A traditional live food for aviary birds is the mealworm *(Tenebrio molitor)*, which is the larval stage of the meal beetle's lifecycle. They are about 31 per cent fat and 56 per cent protein. Mealworms are usually sold by weight in small containers. When you get them home, spread them out in a dry food, such as chicken meal, in a clean plastic container with air holes pierced in the lid.

Mealworms are ideal for larger birds, such as glossy starlings, but beware of feeding them to waxbills and other small birds, including chicks, as they contain an outer casing of chitin, which young birds cannot digest easily. If parents feed mealworms to their offspring, the food may pass through their bodies in an undigested state. The chicks can soon become starved, in spite of being fed. Moulting mealworms, which can be identified by their white skins, are a better option for these birds.

Some softbills, such as Indian blue-throated flycatchers (here, seen eating a mealworm), are highly insectivorous.

Live foods from your garden

Foods such as snails can be gathered from the garden, but take care, as they can act as a host for gapeworm. When gathering food in the garden, make sure that it has not been exposed to any chemical treatments.

Setting up a whiteworm culture

Some live foods are not available commercially, which means you will have to breed them yourself using a starter kit. Whiteworms *(Enchytraeus)* are particularly nutritious and are valuable in the breeding period, as they are readily eaten by adult waxbills and can be easily digested by young chicks.

Whiteworm cultures are easy to establish, and there is no risk of the whiteworm escaping into your home.
• Gather a clean, empty plastic container, complete with lid, and puncture several ventilation holes across the top of the lid.
• Fill the container with dampened peat substitute rather than soil, which is prone to mould and becomes overrun with mites or other soil-borne creatures.
• Soak some stale bread in milk as food, and insert pieces into small holes made with a pencil in the soil.
• Divide up the starter culture and place it on top of the soaked bread. Cover it with some peat substitute.
•Place the lid on the container and keep it in a moderately warm place.
• Check regularly that the top layer does not dry out and renew the food supply as necessary.

WARNING

Molluscs, such as snails, can act as an intermediate host for parasites, such as gapeworm *(Syngamus trachea)*. It is impossible to distinguish visually between those that are healthy and those that pose a threat. When the parasites have completed their development in the bird's gut, they cluster at the entrance to the trachea. This obstruction to the airways could cut off the air supply when the bird is handled or distressed. Infected birds begin gasping, especially with an open, gaping bill. Look out for symptoms particularly in softbills that have recently fledged and are known to have been fed on snails during rearing, and ask your vet for advice.

Home-grown foods

Vegetables, fruit, and other plants are an important source of vitamins and minerals and constitute a valuable part of many birds' diets. In recent years, concern over the use of pesticides has seen a rapid growth in organically raised products, but these foods can be expensive to buy especially when they are out of season. An obvious solution is to grow some of your own fresh food.

VEGETABLES
Many useful food crops for both humans and birds can be grown easily, even in a small garden. If you normally grow your own vegetables, it is often worth planting an additional row in your vegetable garden to provide some extra food for your birds.

Parrots and even some softbills, such as touracos, will eat peas both in and out of their pods, while maize is popular with conures and many neo-tropical parrots. This cereal is less easy to grow in cooler climates as it needs warmth and plenty of sun. Choose a variety that best suits the prevailing climate and, in a sheltered site, sow the seeds in blocks to ensure successful pollination, as the cobs may not develop properly in poor summers.

Spinach beet
Spinach beet, which is more robust than leaf spinach, grows well in any soil, and tolerates dry summers. It is also able to survive frosts, and so can be fed to birds, such as parrots, during the winter months, when other greenstuff is in short supply. Choose a variety that has a low oxalic acid content, since this chemical may interfere with the absorption of calcium from the gut.

When harvesting your crop, pick the leaves from the outside of the plants first, being careful not to uproot them at this stage. Some birds prefer the leaves, whereas others eat the stalks. You can reduce any wastage by slicing the leaves into strips, as they are likely to be dropped on to the floor when offered whole.

Carrots
Although they are difficult to grow successfully in the garden, carrots are a valuable source of vitamin A. Sequential sowings of carrot can provide a steady supply into the autumn months. Choose a modern strain that is resistant to carrot fly, and sow in a site that is free from stones. Thin out plants to ensure large roots. The whole plant can be fed to birds, after the carrot has been scrubbed thoroughly.

WEEDS AND SEEDS
In addition to cultivated vegetables, your birds are also likely to relish wild plant species, many of which are regarded as weeds and not welcomed in gardens. If they are grown in a container, however, these plants are unlikely to cause a problem.

spinach leaves are best sliced into strips

carrots are a good source of vitamin A

apples can be stored as winter food

grapes can be offered whole

Fresh fruits and vegetables can easily be grown or bought when in season.

Chickweed *(Stellaria media)* is popular with many birds. It thrives in a damp, sheltered site such as a greenhouse floor, but avoid using any location where chemical treatments have been used. Harvest the leaves regularly, to stop straggly growth and to help keep the plant bushy.

Dandelion *(Taraxacum officinale)* is especially popular with canaries, and can be grown easily from the tap root of an existing plant. With careful planning, you can raise greenstuff and seed heads through into late autumn in temperate areas.

dandelion leaves are enjoyed by canaries

chickweed can be used as a tonic

Seed providers

The long seed heads of plantain *(Plantago major)* are ideal for drying, and can be fed to canaries and finches in the winter. Teasel *(Dipsacus sylvestris)*, which makes a spectacular plant at the back of a spacious flower border, is also popular with canaries. It can grow to more than 1m (3ft) in height, but the distinctive seed heads do not form until the second year after planting.

Both canary seed and millet can be sown in the garden, taking the seeds direct from stock in your bird room. Only a very small amount of seed is needed to plant a large area; as a guide, about 0.5kg (1.1lb) of seed should cover a plot of 96sq m (120sq yd). Sow in early autumn to allow a long growing period, which should give an increased yield. Cover the seeds with netting to discourage sparrows and mice from eating them. The seed heads ripen to brown in late summer, but they can be cut and fed to birds when they are still green, if needed.

Even plants that are often considered garden weeds can provide birds with a valuable source of vitamins.

Raising sunflowers

Sunflowers are easily accommodated in the borders of a flower garden, provided that the site is sheltered. Check the seedlings regularly, as they are prone to attack by snails and slugs, but this risk lessens once the plants reach about 20cm (8in). Remember to support them with stakes, as they soon become top-heavy when the flower head develops. The cut flower head can be given to birds before it has ripened fully, or you can hang it upside down over a clean surface in a shed, where the seeds can be collected as they fall. These can be stored and fed to birds during the winter months.

FRUITS

The ready availability of fruit in tropical areas ensures a good variety in the diets of softbills and parrots throughout the year. The choice is more limited in temperate regions, but you may be able to find supplies of fruit locally that can be stored for use during winter.

Wild fruits

Blackberries and bilberries are just some of the wild fruits that are readily taken by birds. Choose fruits that are growing in woodland, rather than on roadside verges, where pollution is high. Ignore those growing close to the ground, in case they have been soiled by foxes or other animals, and avoid plants that are likely to have been sprayed with chemicals. If you intend to freeze wild fruits for use through the winter, first remove any stalks, then rinse them well in water. Before use, thaw frozen fruits in a bowl of warm water, as they deteriorate rapidly if left to defrost overnight.

Storing apples

Apples are a valuable stand-by in temperate areas where other fruit is in short supply. Although they do not freeze well, they can be stored successfully. Keep them in a cool place where the temperature is kept above freezing. Select only unblemished fruit for storage, to keep mould at bay, and keep a regular check on the fruits for any signs of rotting. Do not feed mouldy apples to your birds.

FREEZING BERRIES

Freeze the berries as soon after picking as possible, selecting only firm fruits that are unlikely to fall apart when thawed. Rinse the fruits in water, then divide them into small amounts sufficient for daily feeds. Seal them in plastic freezer bags, and place in a freezer. Alternatively, spread the fruits out on a clean tray and freeze. Once frozen, they can be transferred to a plastic container.

Food supplements

Birds fed on a seed-based diet are most likely to require a supplement in their diet to provide the necessary vitamins, minerals, and amino acids. Deficiencies in these can have harmful effects, often resulting in low-quality feathering, poor breeding results, and ill health over a period of time.

CHANGING NEEDS

A bird's nutritional requirements change during its life, and so may its needs for specific micro-nutrients contained in supplements. At egg-laying, hen birds need more calcium which may be provided by cuttlefish or as a prepared supplement. Dietary shortcomings are likely to become evident during the moult, too.

Iodine shortage

Budgerigars have a high requirement for iodine, which is used in the manufacture of hormones that regulate the body's metabolism, and the moult. A deficiency results in enlarged thyroid glands in the neck which, in turn, are likely to press on the windpipe, causing the bird to breathe noisily.

When a bird is deficient, it appears to be stuck in the moult, and the head feathers remain spiky. To avoid this condition, provide an iodine block in the birds' quarters throughout the year. Choose a white rather than a pink

The feed-based diet of budgerigars can lead to conditions such as goitre, which is caused by a lack of iodine.

block, especially if you exhibit your birds, as the pink iodine can leave temporary stains on facial plumage.

TYPES OF VITAMIN

Vitamins are divided into two categories, according to how they are stored within the body.

Water-soluble group • Vitamin B complex and vitamin C are not stored in the body, but filtered out through the kidneys. As a result, they need to be constantly replenished to avoid a shortage.

Fat-soluble group • Most significant are vitamins A and D_3, stored in the liver. If a bird is deprived of these compounds, it can rely on its body reserves for a short period, before a deficiency becomes apparent.

Deficiency in vitamin A

A shortage of vitamin A is the most common deficiency seen in pet birds, especially parrots that have been fed exclusively on parrot seed. It is often heralded by the onset of candidiasis, an opportunistic infection caused by the yeast-like microbe *Candida albicans*. In psittacines, such as grey and Amazon parrots, blocked nostrils suggest an infection in the upper respiratory tract, which can often be linked to a deficiency in vitamin A when the birds have been fed a diet of dry seed. Use a specific supplement based on vitamin A to resolve this shortage, and try to provide a more balanced diet that includes greenstuff and other known sources of vitamin A, such as raw carrots.

Sprinkle powder supplements onto pieces of fruit or damp green leaves so they stick to the food and will be eaten by the bird.

fruit sprinkled with food supplement is readily eaten

Powder supplements

The principle disadvantage of powder supplements, is that they tend to sink to the bottom of the food container when sprinkled over dry seed or are lost when birds discard the outer husks of seeds. To make sure that the supplement is taken by the bird, sprinkle the powder over damp green food or on to the cut surfaces of fruits, so that it adheres more readily.

Softbills generally receive a more balanced diet than seed-eaters, as softbill food or pellets contain essential amino acids, vitamins, and minerals. Those most at risk of suffering from any deficiencies are the insect-eating species, which may be reluctant to take inert foods until they are 'meated off' a diet comprised entirely of invertebrates. Until this stage, powder supplements are needed to raise the nutritional value of their diets, as invertebrates have low calcium levels, relative to phosphorus, and may also be deficient in vitamin A. This technique is sometimes known as 'gut loading'. Either sprinkle powder over the live food, or provide it in supplemented foods that are placed alongside the invertebrates.

Overdosing

Vitamins are only needed by the body in relatively small amounts, such that overdosing can occur even if the supplement has not be given in large quantities. For example, a daily dose of just 0.07 mg of vitamin D_3 given over a short period can be fatal. If a bird is regularly overdosed with fat-soluble vitamins, then toxic side-effects such as diarrhoea and weight loss become apparent; however, the risk of overdosing a bird with water-soluble vitamins is less likely because they are not retained in the body. To avoid harming your bird with an overdose, always read the instructions before using a product. These often differ from product to product, so check carefully if you are changing brands, and avoid using two different supplements at the same time.

USING SUPPLEMENTS

Before using any supplement, look closely at your birds' diet and assess what could be missing. If you are already using a balanced complete food, it may be that a supplement is unnecessary and could even be harmful in the long term. Check the packaging and refer back to the manufacturer if you are not sure. Ultimately, the choice regarding which supplements to offer your birds is a personal one, although it is worth consulting an experienced bird veterinarian for advice if in doubt. Dietary supplements are available in liquid or powder form, both of which are easy to administer.

Liquid supplements

Liquid supplements are generally easy to make up, and birds tend to need little persuasion to drink them. When providing a liquid supplement, it is best to withhold other sources of water, such as fruit and greenstuff, as these may reduce the birds' water intake.

In very hot weather, or when there are chicks in the nest, avoid giving birds a large volume of the supplement and provide them with a drinker of ordinary water to avoid any risk of overdose. Try to position the supplement in a shaded part of the aviary, preferably under cover where it is out of the sun's rays, as exposure to sunlight is likely to reduce its nutritional value as well as encourage algal growth. Wash the container thoroughly at the end of the day and refill it with ordinary water.

GRIT TO HELP WITH DIGESTION

Since birds have no teeth, they depend on their gizzards to crush their food. Grit plays an important part in this process. The rough surfaces of the stones grind up the seeds in the gizzard and prevent particles of food from lumping together. The grit also provides calcium. Oyster-shell grit is more soluble than mineralized grit, so provide a mixture. In the United States, many bird-care experts do not advocate giving grit to birds.

Special diets

A healthy diet is essential to the well-being of your birds. However, a bird's dietary requirements change throughout its life, such as during breeding, through the moult, and as it gets older, and you will need to make adjustments accordingly. Special diets can influence the colour and condition of the plumage and can be used to improve the general health of a bird that is overweight or unwell.

THE MOULT

Most birds moult annually. Moulting allows the old feathers, which can become worn and damaged, to be replaced by new ones. Studies of the increased demands placed on the body by the moult have shown that the energy needs of birds are significantly raised during this period, as their bodies make new feathers. The metabolic rate of finches rises by 30 per cent at this time. By providing high-protein, high energy foods during the moult you can help the bird to develop healthy new feathering. Inadequate feeding will result in poor-quality feathering, marked by barring or even abnormal coloration. In young birds, it can even stunt overall development and growth as all the body resources are used to replenish the plumage.

COLOURING AGENTS

The natural coloration of a bird's plumage can be maintained and enhanced by the use of colouring agents. These products, which are most often used for finches, canaries, and softbills, are commonly available in red, yellow, and orange, and can either be supplied in the form of a special soft food or administered via drinking water. The colouring agent is carried in the blood to the developing feather where it is incorporated, but only while the feather is growing and receiving a blood supply. Once the feather is effectively dead, no colour change takes place, so it is important to start adding the agent before the moult. If you introduce the colour food too late, you may find that the first feathers to emerge are lighter than the rest of the new plumage.

Follow the manufacturer's dosing instructions carefully as overdosing spoils the appearance of the plumage until the next moult. Some exhibitors give colour food once a week throughout the year, just in case a bird undergoes a soft (minor) moult and sheds a few feathers. This can be brought on by a change of temperature between the aviary and a show hall. If the agent has been provided, the new feathers will look no different from the rest of the plumage.

The appearance of some birds alters dramatically following a moult. The large areas of orange plumage seen on the cock bird of this pair of orange weavers show that he is in breeding condition.

hen

cock

The darker, richer colour of the plumage on the colour-fed canary contrasts strongly with the paler plumage of the non-enhanced canary.

non-colour fed canary

colour-fed canary

Balancing the diet

Too many pet parrots are dependent on diets based on sunflower seeds and peanuts, both of which are oil seeds and have a high fat content. Gradually reduce the fat level by introducing more vegetables and fruits. These provide vitamins and minerals, while curbing the parrot's calorie intake. Build up the amount of fresh food until it makes up to half your pet's food intake. Resist giving the many seed-based treats that are now available, and reward your bird with a healthier option instead, such as a piece of fruit or carrot.

CONVALESCENT DIETS

Young birds benefit from a diet of soaked seed, which is softer and more digestible than dry seed. Soaked seed is also useful to rekindle the appetite of sick finches which are reluctant to crack dry seeds.

Special mixtures of seeds intended for soaking are available, although canary seed and millets are popular choices. Avoid making up more than is needed, as any surplus must be discarded within 24 hours. Rinse the seed before placing it in a bowl of hot water, and leave it to stand overnight. Rinse the seed again thoroughly in the morning, and divide it into portions as required. Millet sprays can be treated in the same way.

WATCHING YOUR PET'S WEIGHT

Pet birds are just as vulnerable to obesity as other household pets. To determine whether a bird is fat simply feel the breastbone (see page 9). In obese birds, the usual slight prominence of the bone can be difficult to find. Other indicators of obesity may be poor flight, which can be linked to birds housed indoors having little opportunity to exercise out of their cages. These birds also do not burn up the same amount of energy to keep warm, compared with their aviary counterparts.

Related problems

The combination of weight increase and perches with a constant diameter can make birds prone to 'bumble-foot', in which pressure points on the foot become inflamed, giving rise to painful sores. These make the bird reluctant to put its weight on the affected foot.

Overweight budgerigars are also at greater risk from fatty tumours called lipomas. While these can often be removed by surgery, recurrences are not uncommon.

Regular exercise

Give your pet the opportunity to become more active by providing a flight with plenty of flying space. Place the perches as far apart as possible and site the food and water pots at opposite ends. You may find that birds that have been kept in cages tend to perch mainly in one place, when first released into a flight. This is normal behaviour, but will soon be overtaken by the bird's natural curiosity to explore its surroundings. You will find that the bird's fitness gradually increases, especially if a flying companion is cautiously introduced at a later stage. A similar management programme can be used to prevent pet birds from becoming overweight.

Pet budgerigars are more prone to lipomas than aviary birds. These fatty growths can emerge almost anywhere on the body. They may be linked with a poor diet and lack of exercise.

Hygiene and health

Within the close confines of an aviary disease among birds can spread rapidly, so good hygiene is essential. Besides understanding behavioural problems, you need to be aware of signs of illness and know how to control pests and parasites, infections, and viruses yourself – and when to seek help from a vet.

How diseases spread

When disease strikes, it is often hard to find the source of the infection. It might already have been present in the aviary, or it could have been introduced by a new bird. Stress can increase a bird's susceptibility to illness. For this reason, it is a good idea to quarantine any newly acquired birds and those returning home from shows, keeping them apart from the rest of your collection for at least two weeks.

New birds are particularly prone to illness as a result of encountering unfamiliar microbes in the new environment to which the resident birds are immune. Provide plenty of drinking water and a probiotic to stabilize the beneficial bacteria in the gut .

POSSIBLE SOURCES OF INFECTION

When an outbreak of illness occurs in an aviary, there is always a possibility that you could have infected the birds yourself. Perhaps your hands were dirty when you prepared their food, or you may have unknowingly carried the infection on your clothes or footwear, possibly after attending a show. Once you have walked into the aviary wearing these clothes, the disease is introduced and can be picked up by birds feeding on spilt food on the floor. One way to prevent against this type of infection is to invest in a cheap pair of shoes that you wear exclusively in the aviary.

Aviary visitors

Wild birds that perch above the flight are a common source of infection, as their droppings fall through the mesh. An effective deterrent against these visitors, is to cut back any overhanging branches on which they can perch. If you use branches for perching in the flight, always makes sure that they are washed well before being put into use, in case they have been contaminated by the droppings of wild birds.

Rodents (see pages 60–1) are frequently tempted into the aviary by the prospect of finding food and are responsible for the introduction of a wide range of unpleasant diseases. To discourage them, make a habit of feeding your birds in the shelter rather than the flight, so that their food is less accessible or obvious. As winter approaches in temperate areas, keep a watch for signs of mice and rats entering the aviary. Cut back overgrown vegetation around the base of the aviary so that you can easily see signs of any tunnelling into the aviary and spot would-be intruders.

Bacteria from decaying foodstuffs

Bacteria and mould thrive on rotting food, of which there is invariably a supply in an aviary at the end of each day. Unless this debris is cleared away daily, it could become a source of illness among your birds. As part of your daily routine you should aim to:
• provide small offerings of food at regular intervals, rather than serving one large amount to last the day

---

THE IMPORTANCE OF GOOD HYGIENE

Good hygiene does not eliminate bacteria and produce sterile surroundings, but it does keep their numbers in check so that a bird's body defences are not overwhelmed by microbes. Soiled containers allow bacteria to multiply, so always wash pots, drinkers, and other food containers at least once a day. Those used for perishable foods such as nectar may need more frequent cleaning. The risk of disease is highest in the flight, where birds are housed together. Soil- or grass-covered surfaces provide a breeding ground for infection so you may want to consider a concrete floor for improved hygiene and ease of cleaning.

droppings from wild
birds can contaminate
the aviary interior

dirty perches can
cause foot infections

damaged mesh
can cause injury
to the birds

leftover food harbours
moulds and bacteria,
any water contaminated
by droppings represents
a serious threat to the
birds' health

overgrown borders
conceal where mice
enter by tunnelling, or
through the damaged
mesh

*Spilt food and broken
mesh are an open
invitation to rodents
and wild birds.*

through, especially in hot weather when food
deteriorates quickly;

• clear away any unwanted food, making a note
to reduce the quantity of any particular types of food
that frequently appear in the leftovers;

• discard any food that remains surplus after 24 hours
and replace it with a freshly made batch.

Wet seed can rapidly become mouldy, so keep your
supplies in the shelter where it is dry, and try to place
it in a covered area of the flight when serving it to birds,
so that it is sheltered from rainfall. Dirty seed is also
a threat to the health of your birds, so be wary of seed
that is offered at a low price and only buy stocks from
a reputable supplier (see pages 84–5).

Fresh foods such as nectar and fruit represent
a health hazard in aviaries if they are left in direct
sunlight where they will quickly start to rot. As decay
sets in, there is also an increased likelihood of the food
attracting wasps or flies into the aviary. Both groups
of insects can introduce disease, and it is not unknown
for birds to be stung by wasps. Cut plums and grapes
are particularly attractive to wasps.

Parasites

Parasites build up very rapidly in aviaries, where
their huge reproductive potential makes them
a serious threat to birds. When a female roundworm
produces many thousands of eggs in the wild, these
are scattered over a wide range as the bird moves
through its territory. In an aviary, however, the eggs are
concentrated in a limited area, making the likelihood of
reinfection almost inevitable. Ground-feeding birds,
such as Australian parakeets, are particularly prone to
parasitic infection through eating contaminated food.

Prevention is the best solution to parasitic illnesses,
so always screen and if necessary treat newly acquired
birds, for roundworm. During the isolation period it is
also advisable to spray birds with a special avian
aerosol to kill mites and other external parasites before
releasing them into their permanent quarters.

WARNING

When selecting a perch for your aviary avoid any
branches that are heavily coated with algal growth,
varying in colour from green to black. This
contamination could prove harmful if ingested by
birds such as parrots that have a tendency to gnaw
their perches. Rotten branches, which are likely to
contain fungal spores, are also potentially dangerous.

Recognizing signs of illness and seeking help

Keen observation is a vital skill for successful bird-keeping. It can help you to determine which birds are likely to prove compatible, and also to recognize when a bird is off-colour. Knowing your stock is especially important, because you can detect any behavioural changes at an early stage.

One of the first indicators of illness is that a sick bird is slightly less active than usual. For example, when you enter the aviary, the majority of birds will fly off,

but if one is sick it is likely to lag behind. On closer inspection you will probably be able to see that its plumage is slightly less sleek than that of its companions – a further sign of potential ill health.

Taking the time to look at your birds each day is especially important with finches, as signs of ill-health can easily be overlooked in a planted flight. A sick bird may be hidden in vegetation, particularly when pairs are breeding, and so you assume that all is well.

RECOGNIZING SYMPTOMS

Being able to identify a bird that is off-colour at an early stage may prove vital in saving its life. Although birds are normally healthy once established in their quarters, their condition can deteriorate very rapidly if they fall ill. Listed below are the most common illnesses seen in birds and the appropriate action to take.

Bird group	What to watch for	Action
Finches	• Overgrown claws • Pasting around vent	Arrange to clip claws back. Indicates digestive disorder; antibiotics may be required.
Canaries	• Swelling, possibly feather cysts • Persistent preening	Alter breeding programme. Treat for mites or lice.
Softbills	• Aggressive behaviour at start of breeding period • Swollen abdomen; some difficulty in flying	Remove cock bird for a time, and trim his feathers to prevent injury to hen. Possibly iron storage disease; modify diet; avoid dry fruits.
Budgerigars	• Green droppings • Swollen crop and retching • Coral-like growths around beak • Chicks lose flight feathers – French moult	May need treatment with an antibiotic. Treatment for trichomoniasis. Scaly face: treat with proprietary remedy or ivermectin. Viral illness; thoroughly disinfect quarters; no treatment available.
Cockatiels and parakeets	• Loss of condition; chicks may die soon after fledging White roundworms visible in droppings	Deworm birds and disinfect aviary to kill worm eggs here, which could reinfect the birds.
Parrots and cockatoos	• Feather loss, flaking of bill and claws	Arrange test for PBFD. Infectious, and no treatment available. Keep affected birds strictly isolated.

LOSS OF APPETITE

Keeping a check on the contents of the food pots is often recommended as a means of ensuring that your birds are healthy, but this is not always a reliable indicator. If a group of birds is housed in a flight, especially during the breeding season when rearing foods are also being provided for chicks, it is hard to establish whether a bird has been eating properly.

A combination of loss of appetite and dehydration frequently kills birds which otherwise could be saved. Thanks to advances in veterinary care, the serious risk posed by loss of appetite and dehydration can be overcome by using specially formulated feeding products. Many sick birds die simply because they have lost their appetite, rather than because the medication has failed, so these feeds sustain a sick bird that is not eating, until treatment takes effect. It is always useful to have feeds of this type to hand, although an electrolyte can be used in an emergency.

TREATING BIRDS

Accurate diagnosis of bird ailments is difficult, and invariably requires laboratory tests. However, if a bird is suffering with an infection, you may well need to start a course of treatment without being certain of the cause. This should help to prevent further deterioration in the bird's condition, while special feeding supplements prevent it from becoming any weaker.

When using antibiotics (or other drugs), follow the manufacturer's instructions carefully and ask your vet

It is important to keep a sick bird warm. Larger birds should be isolated and warmed by an infra-red lamp next to the cage.

CHOOSING A VET

When it comes to choosing a vet, seek out a practice that has vets who are experienced in the treatment of pet and aviary birds. Ask locally, among fellow bird-keepers, or even contact practices in advance of needing to use them, so that you can feel secure in calling on their expertise in an emergency. It helps to know where to turn if the worst happens and this may prove valuable in assisting a bird's recovery.

---

for advice if you are in any doubt. Do not be tempted to make the solution stronger than recommended for water-soluble powders, and never stop treatment before the end of a course, even if the bird appears to have recovered fully, as infection might re-emerge.

Once the course is completed, discard any remaining medication and do not use it on other sick birds, because it may be inappropriate. Antibiotic powder may be kept in dry conditions, preferably in a clean, sealed storage jar and placed out of sunlight.

Hand-feeding a sick bird

If you need to feed a sick bird by hand, place the food into a suitably narrow tube and pass it down the throat into the crop. Take care to avoid the windpipe, the opening of which is at the back of the mouth, in the floor of the throat. If fluid does accidentally enter this passage, it is likely to prove fatal, so seek advice from your vet immediately. The first time you try feeding in this way, ask an expert to supervise you.

Isolation quarters

Finches and other small birds are especially vulnerable to chilling if they are not taking enough food. Hypothermia alone can kill them before infection takes hold, so it is important to transfer sick birds from an aviary into a hospital cage or other warm environment to improve the likelihood of recovery.

While ready-made hospital cages are suitable for small birds, parrots and large softbills are more easily housed in a standard cage with an infra-red lamp suspended overhead or placed next to the cage front. When choosing an infra-red lamp, opt for a dull-emitter model that gives out heat rather than light, and which is fitted with a controller to regulate the heat output. The lamp is best positioned at one end of the cage, so that the bird can move away from the heat source when necessary. As the bird recovers from its illness, the heat can be lowered to room temperature.

Dealing with bacterial ailments

Birds can be hosts to many different types of bacteria but, thankfully, the advent of antibiotics has helped to reduce the threat posed by those that are potentially harmful. Even so, vigilance is necessary, because a bird's condition can deteriorate very rapidly when it is suffering from a bacterial ailment.

SEASONAL HAZARDS

Some health problems associated with bacteria are more common at certain times of the year. It is vital to pay close attention to hygiene especially during warm weather, when bacteria are likely to multiply more rapidly. Some bacteria, such as *Escherichia coli*, can double in number every 20 minutes. Replace perishable foods such as egg food twice a day if necessary, to ensure that a fresh supply is available once the chicks have hatched. Replace and wash all food containers at least once a day, and remove any soft food that has been spilt on the floor.

"SWEATING" BIRDS

Canary breeders often refer to a condition seen in canary hens that is known as 'sweating'. These birds are suffering from a potentially fatal enteric infection that produces wet droppings around the nest pan. Once it has become established in an adult bird,

there is a strong likelihood that the infection will be passed on to the chicks. If affected, the offspring are highly vulnerable to dehydration and should they develop diarrhoea they will be even harder to save than adult birds. The treatment is a combination of antibiotics and electrolytes.

YERSINIOSIS

A common problem during damp weather, yersiniosis often proves to be fatal in birds. It is also referred to as pseudotuberculosis, because the white spots visible on the bird's liver at post mortem are similar to those caused by avian tuberculosis.

Variation in symptoms

The signs of yersiniosis vary widely, depending on the type of birds affected, so it is not really practical to give a catalogue of symptoms for its diagnosis. For example, in toucans and other softbills, this infection results in sudden death with few if any preceding signs. In contrast, when canaries are affected by yersiniosis, they frequently develop a chronic form of the illness. Their appearance becomes dull, their feathers fluff up, and they lose weight, but these signs can each be associated with a number of other health problems, not all of which are infectious.

ANTIBIOTIC SENSITIVITY TEST

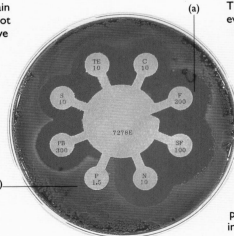

Although antibiotics provide the main means of treating bacterial illness, not all of these drugs are equally effective against particular organisms. Your vet can carry out an antibiotic sensitivity test, to help establish which drug to use, based on the illness identified. It also highlights where an infection has acquired resistance to the antibiotic, so that a less obvious choice can be used to counter that particular outbreak. When several birds are known to have have been in contact with an infected individual, samples (usually faecal) should be submitted for an antibiotic sensitivity test.

The bacterial sample is spread evenly over the special cultural medium in the laboratory. Placed on top is an antibiotic sensitivity disc, containing different antibiotics spread out in a ring. The test is then left for 48 hours to obtain a result. The most effective antibiotics produce a clear area (a) between the arm of the disc that is impregnated with the drug and the resulting bacterial growth. In other cases, the whitish bacterial growth encircles the antibiotic disc (b), suggesting that this particular drug would be ineffective in combating the infection.

Preventing the disease from spreading

Any bird that appears to be off-colour should be removed from an aviary without delay. This is especially critical in canaries and finches, which are housed together in groups, where disease can spread very quickly, especially via contaminated seed and water pots. The source of the infection also needs to be investigated. Yersiniosis may be spread by wild birds that visit the aviary, or by mice that succeed in entering the aviary in search of food.

Establishing a cause of death

If your bird dies from unknown causes, it is very important to investigate by means of an autopsy. Otherwise, the cause of death will remain unclear, and other birds that remain untreated are likely to die as a consequence.

Your vet will be able to undertake or organize the autopsy for you, but in order to give the best results, you will need to arrange for the bird's body to be taken to the veterinary practice in a sealed plastic bag as soon as possible after death occurred. It may be possible to determine the likely cause of death from characteristic changes in the body organs, such as the spots associated with yersiniosis but, in most cases, further tests are recommended.

EYE AILMENTS

Inflammation of the eye is one of the most common minor bacterial infections encountered in birds. Where both eyes are affected, however, this is more indicative of a pox virus (see page 103) or other generalized infection which may not even be of bacterial origin. The first signs are swelling of the eyelids and a discharge, followed by the eye being kept closed.

Eye problems in budgerigars

Budgerigars are especially susceptible to localized eye infections, possibly because one of their characteristic traits is to wipe the sides of their faces along perches. It is often quite difficult to notice an eye ailment at an early stage, as birds often try to conceal the problem by watching you with the unaffected eye. Once you make a closer inspection, though, you will notice that the peri-orbital skin around the eye is clearly inflamed.

Treating infected eyes

Once you recognize that a bird has an eye infection, you will need to house it in a hospital cage for the duration of treatment. Medication may need to be

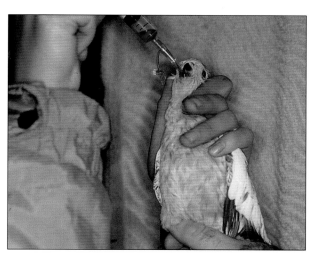

Large birds can be dosed using a crop tube, which is carefully passed down the bird's throat into the crop itself.

given four or more times per day, as tear fluid dilutes its strength. Recovery is likely to be rapid, but continue the treatment as instructed to avoid recurrence.

Using eye drops

Drops are easier to apply than ointment, but tend to be washed out quickly by the eye. If the bird blinks just as the medication is being given, the solution may be scattered over the feathers and will not reach the site of the infection. The principal advantage of drops, however, is for exhibition birds as they do not mat the feathers like ointments.

Eye ointment

The drawback of ointment is that it can stick in the tube, although the flow can usually be eased by running warm water over it. Squeeze the ointment out in a strip across the affected eye, holding the bird for several moments afterwards so that the medication can start to dissolve at the site, rather than being wiped off immediately on to a perch.

After the treatment – the prognosis

Once you have completed a course of treatment, discard any unused medication. You should also replace or disinfect the perches, as the bird may have wiped the discharge here and it could be a hazard to others. The infection is more likely to be local than general, if one eye is affected. Once recovered, relapses are rare and the bird suffers no long-term effects.

Viral infections

While antibiotics have helped to control many bacterial diseases that were once fatal to birds, they have proved ineffective against viral ailments. The key difference between these two groups of microbes is that bacteria multiply independently in the body, so their development can be blocked by drugs without generally affecting vital body processes, whereas viruses take over the nucleus of the living cell in order to multiply. Any attempt to destroy the virus is likely to destroy the cell too, so preventive vaccines are strongly recommended, as these activate the body's own defence mechanisms to recognize and eliminate the virus before it can invade the cells.

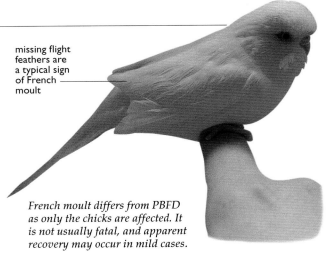

missing flight feathers are a typical sign of French moult

French moult differs from PBFD as only the chicks are affected. It is not usually fatal, and apparent recovery may occur in mild cases.

FRENCH MOULT

The scourge of budgerigar breeders, French moult is a viral illness that affects the bird's feathering. It does not generally kill birds, but it can seriously handicap them by preventing them from flying. The illness is essentially confined to budgerigars, although similar symptoms have been described in a few other members of the parrot family, including peach-faced lovebirds.

Symptoms

Even though they may appear to be quite healthy, older birds carrying the virus, often bring the infection into a stud. However, signs of the illness can usually be seen on closer inspection of the flight feathers. In a normal, healthy feather the pink blood supply that nourishes them is clearly visible in the shaft. However, if a bird is suffering from French moult, traces of dried, rust-coloured blood can usually be seen close to the base of the feather shaft.

WARNING

When cleaning out the aviary, especially after the discovery of a viral infection in one of the resident birds, it is advisable to wear a protective mask over your nose and mouth, of the type sold by pharmacies and hardware stores. Cleaning stirs up feather dust from inside the shelter and flight that could at the very least make breathing difficult. Some bird infections can also affect humans and although the risk is low, it is wise to be cautious. If you do not wear gloves, be sure to wash your hands thoroughly afterwards.

How it spreads

French moult has been linked with an avian polyomavirus that is readily spread by feather dust. Therefore, if a case of French moult emerges in your aviary, you need to eliminate the infection as soon as possible. Carefully clean all nest boxes to prevent transmission of the infection from one nest to another. It is also a good idea to place an ionizer in the bird room to reduce the overall level of aerial pollution, and thereby lessen the spread of the virus.

PBFD

During the 1970s, it became apparent that various cockatoos were being affected by a progressive feather disease, which also attacked the bill, causing it to soften, as well as the claws. Today, psittacine beak and feather disease (PBFD) has been recorded in more than 42 different species of parrot. Unlike French moult, the condition of affected individuals declines progressively, resulting in death. Although a vaccine has now been developed for PBFD, it is not yet available worldwide, because of test protocol requirements. A reliable diagnostic test for PBFD is, however, widely available.

How does PBFD spread?

The virus is thought to be present in faeces, as well as feather dust which can be spread via air currents, rapidly infecting other parrots in the vicinity. The PBFD virus survives well in the environment and is highly infectious. Even aviary equipment, such as nets and gloves can be a source of the disease. Some birds can carry the virus for long periods without developing clinical signs themselves, while remaining a hazard to others. When death does occur, it is usually the result of a secondary bacterial or even a fungal infection, which the body is unable to combat because the PBFD virus has weakened the bird's immune system.

PACHECO'S PARROT DISEASE
Pacheco's parrot disease, which was first described in 1930 in a group of Brazilian parrots, is a herpes virus infection that can infect a wide range of birds. When the disease strikes, it often brings about rapid death, but it produces few tell-tale symptoms other than yellowish diarrhoea in some cases. The main risk for bird-keepers is that some species of conure, including Patagonian conures, can be symptomless carriers of the infection. If one of these is introduced to a new location, it is likely to start shedding the virus, via its droppings. Consequently, when it is housed alongside susceptible species, an outbreak of the illness can be expected. It is impossible to rule out that a conure is not a carrier on the basis of a single faecal examination, because the virus is only excreted on an intermittent basis. The risk is in imported conures, although a recent vaccine has now helped to reduce the incidence of this disease.

OTHER VIRUSES
The number of viruses that may affect birds are far too numerous to mention! There are, however, a few which, although rarely encountered, are worth knowing about.

Newcastle disease
One such virus, called paramyxovirus type 1 (PMV-1), or Newcastle disease, is of major concern because it can be spread from imported cage and aviary birds to poultry flocks – which is why so many countries insist on quarantine periods.

Advice on the movement of birds can usually be obtained from the government department with responsibility for agriculture. Newcastle disease, often called fowl pest when it affects poultry, causes a catastrophic fall off in egg production and frequently results in serious neurological problems for the affected bird.

Pox viruses
Pox viruses sometimes emerge in warmer parts of the world. They are commonly spread to aviary birds by biting insects such as mosquitoes. Canaries are often affected by this pox, and signs of the illness can usually be seen between 3 and 16 days after the initial bite. Signs of infection are swelling around the bird's eyes as well as on its legs, and severe respiratory distress. The mortality rate for this type of virus is variable, because some strains are milder in their effects than others, but those birds that survive this infection acquire a lifelong immunity.

How do pox viruses spread?
Once the infection is present in the aviary, it can be transmitted by contamination of the perches, where canaries have rubbed their heads to ease the irritation. After an outbreak, thorough cleansing is essential, because the pox virus can thrive in the environment, and is difficult to eliminate. After cleaning the aviary thoroughly, apply a phenolic disinfectant to combat the virus. In areas where birds could be vulnerable to pox viruses, a vaccine scratched on the underside of a bird's wing is available for use.

MACAW WASTING DISEASE
Macaw wasting disease, also known as proventricular dilatation syndrome, is a serious concern for breeders of large parrots. Affected birds become depressed and pass seeds undigested. The cause is unknown, but it seems to be a viral disease that dilates the proventriculus (shown below), which grinds up the seed with its muscular action. No treatment is available, and the outcome is usually fatal. It can be spread with the bird's droppings or by regurgitated crop contents.

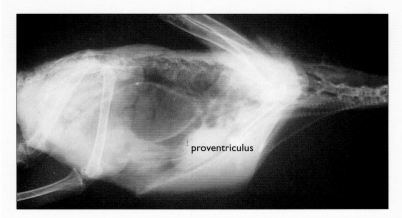
proventriculus

Parasitic problems

Bird parasites can be broadly divided into two categories: those that live outside the body on plumage or skin, such as lice and most mites, and those found within the body, such as intestinal worms.

AIR-SAC MITES

These microscopic parasites live in the birds' respiratory system and are passed from adult birds to their chicks in the nest. Look out for birds that wheeze after they have been flying, or slightly part their bills when resting. These are typical signs of an air sac-mite infestation. Gouldian finches are regularly reared under Bengalese foster parents to eliminate the risk of passing on this disease, although treatment can now be carried out more easily, thanks to the drug ivermectin. Available on veterinary prescription, this is easily administered as drops absorbed into the body through the skin at the back of the neck.

SCALY-FACE MITES

This parasitic ailment is common in budgerigars, and forms nodules over the skin of the body, around the beak, and on the legs. The simplest treatment is to rub petroleum jelly over the affected areas to suffocate the mites. Repeat this process daily for up to 14 days after the signs of infection have disappeared, to be certain of killing off mites that may have just hatched.

If scaly face is left untreated it will destroy the bill.

In more severe cases, where repeated handling could be stressful, ivermectin can be very useful. It is essential to treat scaly face as soon as it is diagnosed to prevent permanent disfiguration of the bird. If left untreated, the damage caused by the mites results in distortion of the beak, to the point that it becomes severely weakened and grows abnormally. The bird will almost certainly need its beak trimmed back regularly for the rest of its life.

RED MITE

The characteristic colour of these parasites, which are barely visible to the naked eye, comes from their habit of sucking blood. This can lead to the spread of microscopic protozoan parasites from one bird to another, often resulting in abnormal weight loss. Unlike lice, the parasites tend to live in dark corners, such as the crevices around the sides of the nest box rather than living permanently on the birds. A heavy infestation of red mites in the nest box can cause severe irritation to chicks, making them restless and anaemic through loss of blood, stunting their growth, and ultimately even killing them.

If you suspect the presence of red mites, cover the cage at night with a white cloth. In the morning, if your suspicions are right, you are likely to find some mites, clearly recognizable as tiny red spots against the white background. To rid your aviary of red mites, use a special aerosol designed for birds. Repeat at fortnightly intervals and, once the chicks have fledged, wash out the entire cage, including the nest box, using a solution to eliminate the mites.

INTESTINAL ROUNDWORMS

These internal parasites are potentially fatal and may cause sudden death in young birds. Fledglings are particularly vulnerable to roundworms, but do not usually show any symptoms of infection until they leave the nest box. They are often found dead on the floor of their quarters or might seem slightly off-colour, before dying unexpectedly.

Treating roundworm

Medication is normally given either in soft food or water. Adult birds are usually treated individually to be certain that each bird has received sufficient medication to eliminate the roundworm. It may be better to move your birds to temporary accommodation such as a large

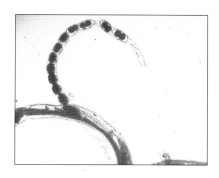

The huge reproductive potential of roundworms can be seen from this microscopic view of a female, showing the long string of eggs in her body.

flight cage when treating them. This enables you to see whether any worms are passed, and allows their quarters to be cleaned. If you are dosing birds in their drinking water, try to do this on a dry day as the bitter taste of the medication may tempt them to drink rain water instead, if a choice is available. Withhold fruit and greenstuff too, because these both have a relatively high fluid content and will reduce the birds' desire to drink.

Reinfection

Dosing simply treats the bird and does not resolve the problem of infection, as roundworm eggs are passed out in the bird's droppings and can quickly reinfect the bird. Australian parakeets are especially vulnerable to these parasites, because they spend long periods foraging for food. The problem is exacerbated by grass floors, because birds nibble at the shoots and, inevitably, swallow some of the worm eggs at the same time. Similarly, infected pairs introduce worm eggs into the nest box, and chicks soon fall victim to the parasites. Second-round chicks are even more vulnerable, because of the higher level of contamination likely to be present in the nest box.

Preventing reinfection

After cleaning the aviary, disinfect the area to destroy the roundworm eggs. It is a good idea to disinfect your rubber boots too, when cleaning, as the eggs can be transferred and spread easily on footwear, as well as on cleaning utensils such as brooms and shovels.

SOURCROP

The microscopic parasite *(Trichomonas gallinae)* that causes the illness known as trichomoniasis or sourcrop, cannot survive for long outside the body. In order for it to live, therefore, it must be passed directly from bird to bird, or transmitted via drinking water. Sourcrop is common in pigeons and doves, and especially in budgerigars, primarily because of their habit of feeding each other, which lends itself to the spread of these parasites. A single infected cock bird can transmit the infection from its upper digestive tract to several hens by feeding them in the aviary at the start of the breeding period. These hens, in turn, are likely to spread the parasite to their mates when paired up in breeding cages. While keeping the sexes apart appears to be the solution, it does not guarantee a slower rate of transmission, because birds of the same gender are also known to feed each other.

Recognizing the symptoms

In many cases, clinical signs of this illness are not obvious. In hens, a dark brown coloration of the cere is likely to be seen, which suggests that the illness could be triggered by hormonal changes during the build-up to breeding condition. Affected birds usually regurgitate mucus which tends to stain the feathering around the bill, and sometimes the forehead. They also tend to spend more time at food pots, but closer examination usually reveals that they have only dehusked the seeds and not actually eaten them. The crop is visibly distended with gas on an affected individual and, if you get close enough, foul smelling. The droppings may be greenish.

Chicks bred from affected budgerigars often show normal growth at first and fledge without problems. In these birds, you are unlikely to detect any obvious symptoms of sourcrop. However, the birds simply starts to fail in health, becoming weaker until it dies.

Sourcrop also strikes finches such as waxbills and munias, but regurgitation of mucus is less common as a symptom of the illness. Rapid treatment is vital to save affected individuals, whatever the species.

RELIEVING SOURCROP

Treatment of sourcrop is reasonably straightforward and can be carried out at home. First, hold the bird upside down, and gently massage out the air and foul-smelling crop contents on to a piece of paper towel. Recovery is then much more likely to be effective, because the discomfort has been eased and the bird can resume eating and drinking again. Its droppings lose their greenish appearance and soon return to normal. Medication given in the drinking water is usually prescribed to treat trichomoniasis, and it is absolutely vital that the full course is given, in order to give the best chance of eliminating the parasite permanently.

Behavioural problems and emergency care

Although not caused by bacteria or viruses, behavioural problems such as feather plucking and aggression can have very serious consequences and are just as much in need of treatment as physical illnesses we have seen earlier in this chapter.

FEATHER-PLUCKING

One of the most common behavioural difficulties encountered in pet parrots is feather-plucking. Some birds, such as the African grey parrot, seem to be more susceptible than others. Unfortunately there is often no easy explanation for this behaviour. Medical problems sometimes underlie cases of feather-plucking, so you might consider a veterinary check-up. You also need to carry out a detailed

Once a parrot starts to pluck out its feathers it may be difficult to persuade it to stop. Regular spraying with tepid water can help to make it preen itself more often.

examination of your pet's lifestyle to understand and resolve the problem before it becomes habitual. Equally, a poor diet may be implicated, as may boredom or sudden changes in the bird's routine or environment.

Bathing

One common cause of feather-plucking in parrots is a lack of bathing facilities. When a bird does not bathe for months, its plumage becomes dull and lacklustre, and no longer lies flat but appears permanently ruffled. In its persistent attempts to smooth out its feathers, the parrot may be driven to pull them out.

If it is not possible to provide bathing facilities, regular spraying with tepid water in a clean plant sprayer is very important (see page 67). The bird will smear its feathers with water-proofing oil from the preen gland, located close to the base of the tail, thus maintaining its sleek appearance. There are special preparations that you can also use to deter a parrot that is already plucking its feathers. They are not always successful, however, and do not deal with the underlying behaviour that caused the feather-plucking in the first place.

PROBLEMS WITH MIRRORS

Cock budgerigars in breeding condition often persist in feeding their reflection in a mirror (see page 21) or attempt to mate with the toys in their cage. While this is a short-term problem that passes, some birds also regurgitate seed to such an extent that they start to lose weight. It is a good idea to remove the mirror as soon as your bird starts to behave in this way, rather than allow the problem to develop particularly if the bird has displayed this habit before.

EMERGENCY CARE

Few things are more distressing to a bird-keeper than losing chicks that have recently fledged, but fatal accidents can happen, especially with birds that become nervous during breeding, such as Australian parakeets, doves, and pigeons.

If on entering the aviary in the morning, you find a young bird on the floor that is alive but appears to have lost its co-ordination, then it might well have suffered from 'night fright' (see page 81), having concussed itself by flying wildly around the aviary and hitting its head after dark.

Budgerigars' bills can become overgrown and require clipping. You can do this yourself, or get your vet to do it for you.

Remove the bird from the aviary disturbing it as little as possible, and transfer it to a cardboard box lined with paper towel and ventilated with adequate holes punched in the sides. Seal the roof with tape and transfer the box to a safe, quiet place. The bird should recover fully within a couple of hours, although there is a real risk of a brain haemorrhage, resulting in death. The skulls of Australian parakeets, in particular, are very thin. Depending on the point of contact, the bone can be shattered rather like an egg shell, and driven into the brain beneath.

CLAW AND BILL CLIPPING

Some birds are likely to need to have their claws trimmed more regularly than others, to prevent them being caught up in the mesh panels of the aviary or plantings. Either get your vet to do this for you, or, if you do it yourself, use a pair of proper nail clippers (as sold for dogs) for this purpose, and not ordinary scissors which are likely to split the nail rather than cutting cleanly through it.

The bill can be trimmed if necessary in a similar fashion, taking care to avoid bleeding,

which is particularly likely when cutting the upper bill. When trimming back an overgrown lower bill, simply cut the overgrown edge back level with the remainder of the bill. With an undershot bill, the bird's beak needs to clipped back regularly. Take particular care though, if the bill is affected by scaly face mites (see pages 106–7) or if the bird is suffering from PBFD (see pages 102–3) as these ailments can weaken its structure, apart from causing it to grow in a distorted fashion.

TREATING FROSTBITE

Following a very cold night where temperatures have dipped below freezing, some birds might show signs of frostbite on the following morning. The most obvious signs are likely to be spots of blood on a perch and if a bird is reluctant to put weight on its feet. Massaging the toes can be beneficial if carried out straight away – it will help to restore the circulation if the injury is not too severe. Dipping the toes briefly in warm (not hot) water may also help.

If these treatments are not effective, the parts of the toes affected by frostbite are likely to shrivel in the course of the next week or so. Ultimately these slough off, sometimes with a little blood loss, but they rarely cause the bird any distress.

To prevent incidents of frostbite in your aviary, try to persuade susceptible species to roost under cover or in a nest box during cold spells of weather rather than on an exposed perch in the open part of the aviary.

TRIMMING CLAWS

Clip your bird's claws in a good light, having first identified the blood supply that runs a variable distance down each claw. If it is cut too short, the nail bleeds, although pressing on the cut end should soon stimulate the clotting process. It is more difficult with dark claws to see the red streak, so err on the side of caution. As long as the hooked end is safely cut off, the risk of the bird getting caught up is greatly reduced. Always use proper nail clippers for this task, and ask your vet for advice if you are unsure.

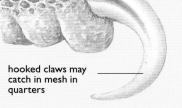

blood supply

hooked claws may catch in mesh in quarters

cut off the tip just above the blood supply

Index

AUTHOR'S ACKNOWLEDGEMENTS
The author would like to thank Rita Hemsley for her help in typing up the manuscript for this book.

PUBLISHER'S ACKNOWLEDGEMENTS
Reed Consumer Books Limited would like to thank the following organizations and people for their help in producing this book:
PAGEOne, (book packagers) Cairn House, Elgiva Lane, Chesham, Buckinghamshire HP5 2JD
Illustrations Anthony Duke 83, 84, Liz Gray 9, 10, 11, 12 17, 49, 50–1, 53, 54, 55, 58–9, 60, 71, 97, 109.
Photography Tim Ridley 6, 56–7, 66–7, 69, 71, 74, 75, 77, 85, 86 (bottom), 87 (top), 88, 90, 91, 93, jacket back.
Symbols Mark Bracey, Karen Cochrane.
Seeds supplied by Ernest Charles & Co, Crediton, Devon.

PICTURE CREDITS
David Alderton 95 (bottom), 100, 102, 107.
Dennis Avon 7, 21, 26, 32, 35 (bottom), 36 (top), 40, 41 (top right and bottom), 42 (top), 44 (top), 45, 47 (bottom), 63, 94, 108.
Bridgeman Art Library London/New York 24 (*Sweet Sounds*, 1918 by John William Godward, 1861–1922, Roy Miles Gallery, London, UK).
Mary Evans Picture Library 22, 25.
Cyril Laubscher 1, 2, 4, 11, 12, 13, 14, 15, 16, 23, 27, 28, 29, 30, 31, 33, 34 , 35 (top), 36 (bottom), 37, 38, 39, 41 (top left), 42 (bottom), 43, 44 (bottom), 46, 47 (top), 61, 64, 65, 68, 72, 76 (top), 78, 80, 81, 86, 87, 89, 92, 95 (top), 99.
Dermod Malley, FRCVS/South Beech Veterinary Surgery 76 (bottom), 101 (reproduced from the *Veterinary Annual* No. 34 (edited by Raw and Parkinson 1994) with permission of Blackwell Science Ltd), 103, 104, 105, 106, 109.
NHPA 18.
University Diagnostics Limited/Barrie Mellars 73.
Bruce Coleman Limited/Jorg and Petra Wegner, Front cover.